CW01649312

ITALIAN LAKES

a countryside guide

Third edition

David Robertson
Sarah Stewart
updated by Sunflower Books

SUNFLOWER BOOKS

Third edition © 2018
Sunflower Books™
PO Box 36160
London SW7 3WS, UK
www.sunflowerbooks.co.uk

All rights reserved. No part of this publication may be reproduced, stored in a retrieval system, or transmitted by any form or by any means, electronic, mechanical, photocopying, recording or otherwise, without the prior written permission of the publishers.

Sunflower Books and 'Landscapes' are Registered Trademarks.

ISBN 978-1-85691-505-2

View from Monte Crocione over Lake Como

Important note to the reader

We have tried to ensure that the descriptions and maps in this book are error-free at press date. The book will be updated, where necessary, whenever future printings permit. It will be very helpful for us to receive your comments (sent in care of the publishers, please) for the updating of future printings.

We also rely on those who use this book — especially walkers — to take along a good supply of common sense when they explore. Conditions can change fairly rapidly in this mountainous terrain, and ***storm damage or bulldozing may make a route unsafe at any time***. If the route is not as we outline it here, and your way ahead is not secure, return to the point of departure. ***Never attempt to complete a tour or walk under hazardous conditions!*** Please read carefully the notes on pages 25 to 29, as well as the introductory comments at the beginning of each tour and walk (regarding road conditions, equipment, grade, distances and time, etc). Explore ***safely***, while at the same time respecting the beauty of the countryside.

Cover photograph: View to Malcesine, Lake Garda (Walks 28 and 29)
Title page: paddle-steamer ferry out of Bellano

Photographs: David Robertson, except for page 3 and cover (Shutterstock)
Maps: Sunflower Books
A CIP catalogue record for this book is available from the British Library.
Printed and bound in England: Short Run Press, Exeter

Contents

Menaggio, Lake Como (Car tours 3 and 4, Walk 12)

Preface

The Italian Lakes have long been a 'must' for holidaymakers, inspired by their dramatic beauty. These great expanses of water, bound to the north by high mountains and stretching down towards the Lombardy Plain, all resulted from glacial activity. This has created distinctive 'micro' landscapes, whereby each lake retains its own character and special aura. While the term 'Italian Lakes' generally refers to Maggiore, Lugano, Como and Garda, there are many other, smaller lakes, some of which we have included on our tours and walks.

Maggiore is the longest of the lakes, and although no dramatic peaks rise from its shoreline, the Val Grande National Park, Italy's most extensive wilderness area, is within easy reach. The three Borromean Islands crown the serene beauty of Maggiore, where only the bustling ferries disturb the tranquillity.

The most romantic of the lakes must be Como, an amazing wishbone shape surrounded by rugged limestone mountains, which contrast with the many fine villas and gardens around its shores. Since Roman times this area has enthralled countless generations, and today it is still the busiest of all the lakes, with the most sophisticated amenities.

Although 60 per cent of Lake Lugano lies in Switzerland, we have included this area, which is easily reached from lakes Maggiore and Como. With fewer resorts than its neighbours, this strangely shaped narrow band of water is remarkably appealing.

Lying apart from the others, Lake Garda is the largest. It stretches from the Lombardy Plain to the foot of the Trentino

View to Monte Generoso from Monte di Tremezzo (Car tour 3, Walks 14, 15)

The bustling ferries

To capture the magic of the lakes you must use the ferries. They ply the waters between the resorts and are comfy and reliable. Steam ferries first appeared on Lake Garda in 1827, but regular services on all the lakes did not begin until the late 19th century. Today diesel power has almost completely taken over from the romantic old paddle steamers (see page 1), which are now mainly reserved for special occasions and evening excursions, a wonderful time to see the illuminated lakeside buildings. For those in a hurry, the hydrofoils *(aliscafi)* go to selected destinations, but are much more expensive.

Top: hydrofoil (aliscafi) *out of Bellano; above: ferry from Varenna*

Dolomites in the north, where mountains rise straight from the shoreline. The lakeside roads here were not built until the 1930s, so tourism arrived much later than at the other lakes. Today it is a sportsman's paradise, the water bright with dancing windsurfers and sailboats.

The superb scenery around each lake offers endless opportunities for outdoor activities. We have gained huge satisfaction from exploring the countryside, where we discovered timeless hill villages, ancient mule tracks and panoramic mountain viewpoints. We hope that you will enjoy our tours and walks and, like us, be captivated by the Italian Lakes.

— David Robertson and Sarah Stewart

Acknowledgements

We are most grateful to the staff at the local tourist information offices that we visited, especially to Mathilde Zuydwegt in Menaggio. Friends and family have once more been full of enthusiasm and encouragement, and we have again to thank Damaris Fletcher for her valuable suggestions. Our thanks go to John Underwood for producing the maps and to our publisher, Pat Underwood, who gave us the opportunity to write about this wonderful area of Italy.

Getting there and getting about

The easiest way to travel to the Italian Lakes is by air. There are airports at Milan from where you can travel by bus or train to your resort on either Lake Maggiore or Lake Como. Some charter flights use the airport at Bergamo (Orio sul Serio), from where Lecco and Como are readily accessible by bus. For those visiting Lake Garda, flying to Verona is the best option, with onward travel by bus. Car rental, available at all the airports and in most large towns, can be pre-booked as a fly/drive deal. There are also local car rental companies, which may be cheaper. Do not discount package holidays — there is plenty of choice to many of the resorts.

Driving to the Italian Lakes is an option and is recommended for those who enjoy the flexibility and freedom of having their own transport. After crossing the English Channel by either tunnel or ferry (there are also ferries from Hull and Rosyth in Scotland to Zeebrugge) it is an easy drive of a day and a half to the lake of your choice. Be aware that to drive on the Swiss motorways you must purchase a 'Vignette' (£32 at press date) either before you leave (contact Switzerland Tourism: www.myswitzerland.com), or at the border. While there are no longer any direct motorail services from Calais or Paris to anywhere in Italy, there *is* one from Düsseldorf to Verona and another to Livorno: check out details at the brilliant website www.seat61.com.

The bus and ferry services around the lakes are excellent, and we have used them to access many of our walks. The local tourist information offices will provide you with up-to-date timetables to supplement the information given on the back of our touring map. In fact the best way to visit the lakeside towns and avoid the busy roads is to use the ferries. However you *will* need a car to explore the countryside above and beyond the lakes and to reach some of our walks.

Santa Maria Maddalena bell tower at Ospedaletto

Picnicking and short walks

The villages around the Italian Lakes afford endless opportunities for eating alfresco. However, it is always fun to leave the busy lakeside and find wonderful viewpoints or peaceful locations for a picnic. Below are our suggestions for ideal places to stop and absorb the beauty all around you. Some are just off the road, while to reach others requires a bit more effort. All are easily accessible, some following one of the walks described in this book for a short distance, others making excellent short walks in themselves.

The location of the picnic is indicated by the symbol ***P*** printed in green on the appropriate walking or touring map, and many of them are illustrated. The symbol ○ indicates a picnic in full sun. **All picnickers should read the Country code on page 29 and go quietly in the countryside.**

Much of Italy's food is perfect for picnics — tasty bread, filled with cheese or smoked meat, along with some vine-ripened tomatoes and olives. Wash this down with some local wine or fruit juice. For dessert, how about a fruit-filled pastry?

1 Santa Anna (*map pages 34-35*)

From Cannobio (Car tour 1) follow signs for Falmenta; turn right after 1.4km for Traffiume and park at the church. Or to Traffiume (four services per day; see inside back cover). 9-12min on foot. Walk across the roundabout to join Via Cressini and take the first turn right. Where this road forks, go right to meet a narrow cobbled street and then Via Torri. Follow this to reach the main village road near an old chapel. Walk on for a few minutes to the little church of Santa Anna (seats, picnic tables). *Picnic here or descend steps to the pebble beach and deep river pools, which are ideal for a cooling dip. An enchanting place from where you can look up to Santa Anna and, from the old bridge, down into the narrow, steep-sided gorge.*

2 Carmine Superiore (*map pages 34-35, photograph pages 36-37*) ○

(Car tour 1) or to Carmine Inferiore (18 services a day; see inside back cover). 15min on foot. Follow Short walk 2 on page 35. *From the balcony of this frescoed church there are superb views across Lake Maggiore to Luino and the mountains beyond.*

3 Piancavallo (*touring map*) ○

(Car tour 1). See 'Transport' for Walk 4 on page 42 and park just below Piancavallo. 10-15min on foot. Walk down the Premeno road for about 200m, to find a path opposite a small layby, which leads up onto the ridge. Wander along the bouldery crest to find your picnic spot. *Incredible views down to Lake Maggiore and across to the Val Grande National Park.*

4 Mottarone or Palestra di Roccia *(map pages 52-53)* ○

🚗 (Car tour 2). Park in the car park below the Mottarone summit. Or 🚡 from Stresa to the top cable car station. Two picnic spots are recommended:

Picnic a: Mottarone summit. This is 5-10 on foot from the car park or 17min on foot from the top cable car station (follow Walk 8 on page 53 to the 17min-point). *Panoramic mountain and lake views from the grassy summit.*

Picnic b: Palestra di Roccia *(photograph page 16)*. From the small gift shop near the car park allow 10-40min on foot; from the top cable car station allow 25-50min on foot. In either case follow Alternative walk 8 (page 52) as far as you like. *A more secluded spot, Palestra di Roccia offers spectacular views over Lake Orta.*

5 Torrente Pescone *(map page 58, photograph page 59)*

🚗 (Car tour 2). Park in Agrano. 31min on foot. Follow Walk 10 (page 58) to the 31min-point. *Picnic on the smooth rocks beside the river pools; take a swimsuit.*

6 Lake Orta — Pella *(map page 62, photograph page 61)* ⛩

🚗 (Car tour 2); park off the main road beyond the church, near the bridge over the Torrente Pellino in Pella. a) 12min on foot. Follow Walk 11 (page 61) to the 12min-point. *Magnificent views across Lake Orta to Isola di San Giulio and along the water to Mottarone.*

b) 40min on foot. Follow Walk 11 to the 40min-point and picnic on the waterfront. *Photograph page 61.*

7 Monte Generoso *(map page 71, photograph page 72)* ○

🚗 (Car tour 3). Park in the railway station car park and take the cog railway to the Vetta station. 35min on foot. Follow Walk 14 (page 71) to the 34min-point and picnic on the grassy top just beyond. *Wonderful views of Monte Generoso and down to Lake Lugano.*

8 Rifugio Venini *(map page 75)* ○

🚗 (Car tour 3). See page 74 and park at Alpe di Lenno. 25-30min on foot. Follow Walk 15 (page 74) beyond Rifugio Venini for as long as you like and picnic on the grassy hillsides beside the track. For a longer excursion return via the Short walk over Monte Calbiga. *A peaceful, pastoral setting in mountain surroundings.*

9 Porta Prada — Grigna *(map page 88, photograph page 89)*

🚗 (Car tour 4). See page 87 and park at Vo di Moncodeno. 41-49min on foot. Follow Walk 20 to the chapel at the 41min-point or to Porta Prada at the 49min-point. *Picnic by the Cappella Votiva or the spectacular rock arch of Porta Prada, on the flanks of the immense mountain bulk of Grigna.*

10 Piani d'Erna *(map page 92)*

🚗 (Car tour 4) or 🚌 from Lecco to the cable car station (see page 92), then take the 🚡 to Piani d'Erna. From here you have two choices. a) Follow Walk 22 to Croce Pizzo d'Erna (8min). *An eagle's-eyrie viewpoint down over Lecco and across to the rugged cliffs of Resegone.* b) Follow *Alternative* walk 22 for 5-10min and picnic on the grassy slopes. *Overlook Piani d'Erna, with Resegone as a backdrop.*

11 Lago del Segrino — Canzo *(touring map)*

🚗 (Car tour 4). Follow Car tour 4 to Lago del Segrino. At the far end of the lake, just before the 'Canzo' sign, turn right and park. 5-20min on foot. Walk along the pedestrianised lakeside road — a fitness trail — and picnic on the banks. *A stretch of the legs and a quiet spot to enjoy a picnic on a sightseeing day.*

12 Monte Falo *(map page 95, photograph pages 94-95)* ○

🚗 (Car tour 4). Follow Car tour 4 or, if driving directly from Bellagio, see page 94. Park at Colma. 8min on foot. Follow Walk 23 to Monte Falo and picnic on this grassy hillock. *A quiet, easy-to-reach picnic spot with extensive views.*

13 Monte Brione *(map page 98, photograph page 98)*

🚗 or 🚌 to Porto San Nicolo, as described on page 98. 12-15min on foot. Follow Walk 25 up to one of several viewpoints. *Lovely views over Torbole and along the length of Lake Garda.*

14 Monte Grande *(map page 106, photograph page 107)* ○

🚗, 🚌 or ⛴ to Malcesine, as described on page 106 (Walk 28). 5-20min on foot. Take the 🚡 to the top station. From the exit turn left and walk up to Monte Grande or further along the Monte Baldo ridge. *Wonderful mountain panorama and views down to Malcesine and across Lake Garda.*

15 Above Malcesine *(map page 109, photograph page 110)* ○

🚗, 🚌 or ⛴ as Picnic 14 (if travelling by bus see also page 109). 28min on foot. Follow Walk 29 to just before the 29min-point. *Picnic on the grassy bank overlooking olive terraces, with a fine view down to Malcesine and its castle.*

16 Monte Bestone *(map page 116, photograph page 115)* ○

🚗 (Car tour 5). See page 115 and park at the Hotel Balzi. 15-37min on foot. Follow Walk 31 up to the viewpoints or the summit of Monte Bestone. *Fine views along Lake Garda and to the surrounding peaks.*

17 Monte Castello *(map page 119, photograph page 120)*

🚗 (Car tour 5) or 🚌 as described on page 119. 26min on foot. (Unprotected cliffs, so unsuitable for children.) Follow Walk 33 to the 26min-point. *Rocky outcrops provide dramatic views down to Lake Garda and back to the Santuario Madonna di Montecastello.*

18 San Rocco, Moerna *(map page 125)* ⛩

🚗 (Car tour 5). Park in the car park below the little cemetery at Moerna. 10min on foot. Walk back down the road towards Persone and, at the first left-hand bend, turn right on a narrow road. Follow this to reach the little church of San Rocco where there is a play area, picnic tables and also plenty of grass to sit on. *Good views over Valvestino and back to Moerna.*

19 The beaches of Lemprato *(touring map, photograph page 23)*

🚗 (Car tour 5). Park beside Lake Idro at Lemprato. 5min on foot. *Picnic on the beach, with lovely views along the lake.*

20 On the shores of Lago di Ledro *(see the touring map)* ○

🚗 (Car tour 5). Either follow Car tour 5, or drive directly from Riva del Garda following signs for 'Ledro' and park at Pieve di Ledro. 5-20min on foot. Walk along the lakeshore towards Mezzolago and pick your spot. *Enjoy the quiet beauty of this small lake.*

21 Pregasina *(map page 131, photograph page 132)*

🚗 (Car tour 5). Either follow Car tour 5 or see Short walk 38 on page 131 for directions from Riva del Garda. 7min on foot. From the car park below the church, walk straight on past the children's play area, along a gravel track. In 6min you will see a 'Fire Danger' sign and a little path going off to the left. Follow this for a few metres to reach a flat grassy area. *Good views along Lake Garda and across to Monte Baldo.*

Touring

The tours we have chosen explore the countryside beyond the lakeshore towns, and here we have found inspiring walks and a great variety of picnic spots. Wherever possible we have avoided the lakeside roads, which are invariably busy. To explore the beautiful resorts around the lake we would recommend using the excellent ferry services, which are a relaxing and scenic way to get about.

All our tours are circular and on each we have started from one base where there is accommodation, but we have also suggested other places where you might like to stay. The tourist information offices which you will find in most of the lakeside resorts are well stocked with brochures, street maps, ferry and bus timetables as well as ideas for local sightseeing. For in-depth historical, botanical and other interesting information you will need a good general guide.

Italian **roads** are of a high standard with good road **signs**, but the locals love to drive fast, and a car in front presents them with a challenge for overtaking. This can be unnerving! However, the roads away from the lakesides are not too busy, so that driving is exciting and enjoyable. Do keep an eye on your petrol tank, as **service stations** can be few and far between and, on Sundays, many are closed.

The pull-out touring maps are designed to be held out opposite the touring notes and contain all the information you need when driving in the countryside. We have endeavoured to give clear directions at all times. In towns, where the route is difficult to follow, our written directions are very specific. At appropriate intervals we have shown the cumulative distance in kilometres and have included an overall estimated driving time. In built-up areas the speed limit is 50km/h; on secondary roads 90km/h; on main roads 110km/h. The *autostrada* (motorway) speed limit is 130km/h. While touring do not expect to average more than 55km/h (35m/h). Allow ample time for stops and extra for any detours. **Symbols** used in the text are explained in the key on the touring maps.

We usually pack a picnic for our excursions, but you will find plenty of places along the way — especially bars, pizzerias and trattorias — where you can stop for a drink or a meal.

All motorists should read the Country code on page 29 and go quietly in the countryside.

Car tour 1, Maggiore: ON THE EDGE OF VAL GRANDE

Cannobio • Cannero Riviera • Ghiffa • Intra • Cambiasca • Aurano • Piancavallo • Premeno • Intra • Ghiffa • Cannero Riviera • Cannobio

80km/50mi; 2.5 hours' driving

On route: Picnics 1, 2, 3; Walks 1, 2, 3, 4, 5, (6, 7)

This short tour leads you away from the tourist towns of the lakeside and high up through the remote villages that dot the hillsides of Valle Intrasca. The amazing views of Lake Maggiore and over the Val Grande National Park are not to be missed, nor is the ambience of this wooded countryside. The road from Ponte Laura to Aurano is narrow, very steep and is not recommended for nervous drivers. It can be avoided by driving the tour in reverse up to Piancavallo and returning the same way. Valle Intrasca can easily be reached from Stresa by driving along the lakeside and then following the tour from Intra.

Leave **Cannobio★** (*i*✝⛰△✕⊕⛽⛩MWC; Walks 1-3, (6, 7); Picnic 1) on the main lakeside road, heading south towards Cannero Riviera. Go through the houses of **Carmine Inferiore** (parking for Short walk 2-2 and Picnic 2) and continue past the ruined island castles of **Castelli di Cannero** (just before you reach them there is a layby on the left). A drawbridge once connected these two Cannero castles, each on a separate island. They have a notorious history. In the 15th century the Mazzarditi brothers terrorised the lakeside inhabitants from this base. When eventually they were captured after a six-month siege, the castles were destroyed.

The main road runs above **Cannero Riviera★**(7km *i*✝⛰△✕⊕WC; Walk 2), but do drive down into this quiet and attractive lakeside town. Elegant villas look out over the waterfront and lovely old houses line the narrow streets. It is renowned for its mild winters and Mediterranean vegetation, hence the name Riviera. A walk by the lake along to the harbour and sandy bay, full of colourful boats, is delightful.

Continue on to **Oggebbio** and down to **Ghiffa★**(15km **M**), famous for its hat-making museum. The road now widens and you soon reach **Intra** (19.5km ✕⛽) which, with its neighbour Pallanza, forms Verbania. Intra has a large Saturday market and is the busiest commercial town on the lakeside. Pallanza (❀) is much more tourist-friendly, with fine villas including Villa Taranto, 20 hectares of botanical gardens with a wonderful collection of exotic plants. Coming to Intra, cross the first bridge, continue along the front and then turn right at the first roundabout, signposted for ARIZZANO and PREMENO. Go straight over the next roundabout, right at the third and fourth (both signed for PREMENO), and left at the fifth, for MIAZZINA (but if you want to drive direct to Il Colle for Walk 4 or Picnic 3, turn *right* here for PIANCAVALLO). Now keep following signs for MIAZZINA (Walk 5) at any junctions/roundabouts.

Just as you enter **Cambiasca** (24km), pick up signs for VALLE INTRASCA, which take you away from the urban area. You now enter the quiet wooded valley of **Valle Intrasca**, passing through the small peaceful village of

Cannero Riviera

Ramello. Beyond you can see Intragna, high on the tree-covered slopes. Go over the **Ponte Nivia** and then turn right for AURANO. Continue through the woods on the narrow road, looking up to Aurano, high above the attractive gorge. You cross the gorge again at the next bridge, **Ponte della Giavina** and, for the final time, at **Ponte Laura** just before the turn-off to Scareno. From here the narrow road climbs out of the valley by a series of vicious hairpin bends to eventually reach **Aurano** (33.5km ✕). This village perches precariously on the hillside, the houses appear as if stacked one upon the other. There is a large car park if you wish to explore this airy settlement.

Follow signs for PIANCAVALLO and continue climbing, now less steeply, through lovely birch woods. When the road eventually levels out, you pass the **Maggiore Zipwire★** — an opportunity for a hawk's-eye view over Valle Intrasca and the lake.

You soon reach a T-junction just below **Piancavallo** (38.5km); opposite is a large parking area (⛩📷; Picnic 3) and a wonderful vantage point overlooking Lake Maggiore. If you turn left here and continue uphill for just 400m you will come to the Auxology Institute (⊕), where the science of human growth in sickness and health is studied. It is a strange place, but there are interesting market stalls there every weekend. (For Walk 4 continue on past the hospital).

The Tour now turns right downhill towards Verbania on a much wider road. Follow the easy hairpin bends and swooping corners, passing through the small hamlet of **Manegra** (✕), and then climb up to **Pian di Sole**. Keep left here, and descend once more to **Premeno** (48km ✕). Follow the short one-way system through this attractive village, which still has many old stone-roofed houses. At the T-junction turn right for Verbania, winding down the hillside to pass through **Bee** (✕⊕), from where there are extensive mountain views, and then on to **Arizzano**.

At the bottom of the hill you cross the Torrente San Giovanni and enter **Intra** (60.5km). Continue a short way to a roundabout where you turn left towards LOCARNO, to rejoin your outward route. Go left at the next roundabout, then straight over the third and on to the lakeside. Here turn left to return to **Cannobio** (80km).

Car tour 2, Maggiore and Orta: MOTTARONE — THE MOUNTAIN OF TWO LAKES

Stresa • Levo • Alpino • Mottarone • Armeno • Agrano • Pettenasco • Orta San Giulio • Gozzano • San Maurizio d'Opaglio • Pella • Madonna del Sasso • San Maurizio d'Opaglio • Gozzano • Armeno • Gignese • Levo • Stresa

116.5km/72mi; 3.5-4 hours' driving

On route: Picnics 4, 5, 6; Walks 8, 9, 10, 11

Mottarone, the backdrop of Stresa, is known as the 'mountain of two lakes'. On this tour we drive to the summit, explore the charming villages on its slopes and discover the serene beauty of Lake Orta, Maggiore's little sister, with its enchanting island and tranquil waters. If you are based in Cannobio and wish to explore Mottarone, Stresa is only 40km/25mi away.

From the ferry terminal in **Stresa**★ (*i*MWC; Walks 8, 9), head north along the waterfront towards BAVENO. Turn left after less than 0.5km (by the Palma Hotel), following signs for GIGNESE. After going under the railway bridge, turn right and then go left at the next junction. In just a few minutes you are away from the bustling lakeside resort and in quiet wooded countryside, with glimpses down to Stresa and across the lake to the Borromean Islands (see panel on page 54). Turn left in **Someraro** and climb up to the narrow streets and terraced houses of **Levo** (6.5km), to continue on an easier gradient, before turning right at a T-junction towards GIGNESE (10km). At traffic lights on the outskirts of this village bear right up a narrow road signposted to GIARDINO ALPINIA and FUNIVIA, At the next junction, follow MOTTA-

RONE to the right, rising quite steeply to an excellent viewpoint in **Alpino★** (📷❀). Pass the turning to the Alpine Botanical Garden, well worth a visit to see and identify the many alpine plants that grow in the Piedmont Alps. After passing a campsite on your left, turn right at a T-junction to enter the **Mottarone Park** — there is a small toll for vehicles. The road zigzags gently upward towards the summit. Turn right at a junction to drive the final kilometre to the car park, ignoring the turn to the cable car station. The summit of **Mottarone★** (23km ⛰▲✕📷⛩; Walk 8; Picnic 4) is just a few minutes' walk away and has wonderful views of the mountains, from the huge bulk of Monte Rosa, the second highest peak in Western Europe, to the Adamello and Ortler Alps in the east. Look to one side to see Lake Maggiore and, to the other, Lake Orta.

Return to the junction below the summit and keep straight on (signed to ORTA and ARMENO). What a panoramic drive! The road winds easily down (📷) and there are plenty of places to park and savour the views. In the narrow streets of **Armeno** (35km ✝), which has a church with wonderful old frescoes, keep right in the one-way system and then turn right in the central square for OMEGNA and BASSOLA. Continue through **Bassola** and **Pescone** to **Agrano** (43km ✕WC; Walk 10; Picnic 5).

Keep on through the village, past the second church, and then descend towards Lake Orta. Turn left (signed to NOVARA) opposite a garage (⛽) on the main road. This road runs along the lakeside, passing **Punta di Crabbia**, from where there is a fine view (📷) over the lake. You next come to **Pettenasco★** (51km *i*✕⛽**M**), which has a very interesting museum of old tools and machines. Some 2.7km further on turn right at the roundabout for ORTA, by the impressive Moorish-looking hotel, Villa Crespi. Drive down to the large car park (metered) at the road's end above **Orta San Giulio★** (55km *i*✝⛰▲△✕⊕📷WC).

Then walk down to this beautiful old town. Situated on a small peninsula, in a most romantic setting, it is full of picturesque cobbled streets with tempting shops and pastel-coloured buildings, many with wrought-iron balconies. The main piazza has attractive cafés and restaurants, all with fantastic views across to the adjacent island village of Isola San Giulio. From the waterfront, ferries run frequently to the island, named after the hermit who spent much of his life there and converted this area to Christianity. There is also a ferry to Pella (Walk 11; Picnic 6).

Isola San Giulio from Orta San Giulio

Top: view to the summit of Mottarone from the setting for Picnic 4b; below: the town hall and Piazza Motta in Orta San Giulio

Head back to the main road and turn right by Villa Crespi, towards NOVARA, to follow the lakeside. Beyond the hilltop tower of **Torre di Buccione** (■) you reach the lake's southern end at **Buccione** and then climb up to **Gozzano** (61km ▲✕⛽⊕). Turn right at the first roundabout following the sign for SAN MAURIZIO D'OPAGLIO. At the next roundabout turn right again, signposted for PELLA. As you drive along look up to your left to see the amazing white church of the Madonna del Sasso, which we visit later. Turn right at the traffic lights in **San Maurizio d'Opaglio** (65.5km ⛽), signposted to LAGNA and PELLA. Bypass Lagna to reach the waterside and enter the attractive lakeside village of **Pella★** (69km ✝△✕📷; Walk 11; Picnic 6). To continue the tour go back a short way and then turn right (signposted to ALZO) by San Filiberto, a pretty church surrounded by shrines depicting scenes from the life of Christ and with an amazing grotto by the door. At the next junction turn right (towards CESARA) and then, at the roundabout, turn left uphill. At the top turn right and then left, signed to BOLETO. Climb the zigzags, make another left turn up a steeper and narrower road, and follow 'SANTUARIO' signs to **Madonna del Sasso★** (75km ✝✕📷WC), a sanctuary built from the remains of a 16th-century chapel. Walk out onto the balcony perched on the high white cliffs for unrivalled views over Lake Orta, Orta San Giulio and across to Mottarone.

Return all the way down the zigzags and follow signs to **San Maurizio d'Opaglio**, from where you retrace your route back to **Gozzano** (87km). Turn left at the first roundabout in the town and then turn right at the junction just over 1km further on towards ARMENO, AMENO and MIASINO. The road passes behind the Torre di Buccione, and there are views to Monte Rosa and down to the lake. Follow the signs to ARMENO through a series of junctions. (You may like to take a detour to Ameno, a village with lovely baroque churches, or to Miasino with its grand villas and delightful gardens, much favoured by 19th-century artists). Do not confuse Ameno with Armeno!

From the outskirts of **Armeno** (96.5km) follow signs for Stresa, driving along the quiet road beside the **Torrente Agogna**, up through an attractive wooded valley dotted with little farms. You pass a large riding centre on your left and, after crossing the deep gorge of the **Torrente Scocia** on a high bridge, you enter **Gignese★** (106.5km ✕⛽**M**). It has an attractive church and an umbrella and parasol museum. On the far side of this town you rejoin your outward route. Not long after leaving Gignese, *make sure that you follow the signs left* for BAVENO/LEVO and then, lower down, follow signs back to **Stresa** (116.5km).

Car tour 3, Lugano and Como: BORDER HOPPING AROUND LAKE LUGANO

Menaggio • Porlezza • Lugano • Bissone • Arogno • Lanzo d'Intelvi • San Fedele Intelvi • Argegno • Ossuccio • Tremezzo • Griante • Menaggio

78.5km/49mi; 2-2.5 hours' driving

On route: Picnics 7, 8; Walks 12, 13, 14, 15, 16, 17, (18)

On this tour we drive beside two delightful lakes, pop in and out of Switzerland, and explore the amazingly beautiful Intelvi Valley that links lakes Lugano and Como.

If you are based in Bellagio or Varenna, take the inexpensive car ferry to Menaggio to join the tour. From **Menaggio★** (***i***✝▲▲▲∆✕⛽⊕WC; Walks 12, 13, (18)) follow signs for LUGANO and PORLEZZA. This busy main road zigzags up behind the town to **Croce** (⛽) and then continues easily through **Val Menaggio**, passing attractive villages and terraced hillsides — mostly abandoned. You go by a nautical museum (**M**) just before **Lake Piano** — a pretty little lake separated from Lake Lugano by a narrow strip of land. This land has been a nature reserve since 1984. Drive through a small industrial area by San Pietro before reaching **Porlezza** (12.5km ▲▲▲∆✕⛽⊕) at the tip of **Lake Lugano**, a lake that is both Swiss and Italian. Keep on the main road on the north side, which affords splendid views down this enchanting lake. You now go through several tunnels.

After **Albogasio** you come to the border, passing first through the Italian customs and then the Swiss, so have your passports ready! (At 21km, ⛽ just across the border in Switzerland).

After more tunnels and some hairpin bends you enter **Lugano★** (27.5km ***i***▲▲▲∆✕⛽⊕🚡**M**WC), a large city situated in a sheltered bay. The tree-lined lakeside promenade has many pretty gardens and, of its several museums, the one devoted to chocolate is perhaps the most tempting! Funiculars run to the summits of Monte Bre and Monte San Salvatore, from where there are spectacular views. Keep beside the lake all the way through the city. The road runs beside the railway, and there are great views across the ever-narrower lake to Monte Generoso (Walk 14, Picnic 7). Eventually you drive under the motorway. Just after, at a roundabout, take the second exit for CAMPIONE, an Italian enclave totally surrounded by Switzerland. Go straight over the next roundabout, then get in the left lane for CHIASSO/BISSONE/CAMPIONE. You cross the bridge that spans the lake.

On the far side, turn right off the roundabout and go through **Bissone** (35km), to follow the lakeside again. Look out for the left turn for AROGNO, which goes under the railway and *autostrada* (but to drive to Capolago and the start of Walk 14, continue straight on here). The Arogno road heads uphill with a good outlook over the lake. Zigzag up through farmland, enjoying the fine views across the valley and the terraced vineyards above Devaggio. There is a layby just by the Arogno entrance sign from where you can clearly see the observatory and summit of Monte Generoso.

On the far side of **Arogno** (42km) fork left uphill on a narrow but attractive road signposted to VALMARA/DOGANA, soon crossing the Swiss/Italian border. About 1.5km further on keep left at a fork. Before long you enter **Lanzo**

Tremezzo

d'Intelvi (49km ▲✕**M**), one of the main tourist centres, popular both with summer visitors and winter sports enthusiasts. Go through the village to a roundabout. For a small diversion (3.5km return) turn left here and then, at the next junction, go right on the road just to the right of the memorial (there is an inconspicuous yellow signpost to BELVEDERE). Past one or two hotels and restaurants, follow the road round to the right (at what looks like a T-junction) — to where it ends after 1.5km. This is **Belvedere** (▲✕📷), which has good parking and a superb balcony viewpoint overlooking Lake Lugano — as well as a few more restaurants.

Return to the roundabout in Lanzo d'Intelvi, where you turn left to leave this prosperous village and drive through the **Intelvi Valley**. This charming, sun-drenched valley that links lakes Como and Lugano, is characterised by interesting pastoral villages and green pastures, protected by 1000m peaks. In former times (and well documented in the local museums), the principal trades were building, stone-cutting and sculpting. Now the prosperity of the area depends almost entirely on tourism and outdoor pursuits. Go straight through **Pellio** (✕), where the road is very narrow and, ignoring a left turn for Laino and Menaggio, carry on through **San Fedele Intelvi** (55.5km ✝✕), another busy town with a lovely church (turn left here for Walk 15 and Picnic 8).

From here you start to descend in zigzags down the steepening valley, with wooded slopes on either side. Keep left for ARGEGNO and COMO, passing through **Castiglione** (♜▲✕⛽), where there are some interesting old houses and the ruins of an ancient tower. At **Muronico**, you will see Lake Como ahead. Turn left in **Argegno** (64km ✝✕; Walk 16), passing its pretty church and red-tiled houses, to start your drive alongside beautiful **Lake Como**. The stunning mountains at the north end of the lake are in full view. Drive through the villages of **Colonno**, **Sala Comacina** and **Ospedaletto** (✝), famous for the church of Santa Maria Maddalena, with its picturesque bell tower (shown on page 7). Just beyond is **Ossuccio** (69.5km ✝♜✕), where Walk 16 ends. Drive past **Lenno** (⛽), which reserves its beauty for those who investigate the lakeside promenade, and **Portezza** to arrive at **Tremezzo** (73.5km ▲✕⛽❀**M**). Stop here to visit the grand Villa Carlotta, with its ornate rooms, fascinating art collection and luxuriant gardens. The road now closely follows the shore to pass by **Cadenabbia** and **Griante** (Walk 17), then continues for a further 5km back to **Menaggio** (78.5km).

Car tour 4, Como: VALSASSINA AND THE TRIANGOLO LARIANO

Menaggio • Varenna • Esino Lario • Cortenova • Introbio • Ballabio • Laorca • Lecco • Pusiano • Canzo • Asso • Sormano • Colma • Zelbio • Nesso • Bellagio • Menaggio

112km/69.5mi, plus two car ferries; about 3 hours' driving

On route: Picnics (9), 10-12; Walks 12, 13, (18), 19, (20), 21-23, (24)

From the ancient town of Varenna, this tour heads east to discover the green valley of Valsassina, bounded in the west by the towering Grigna range. We briefly rejoin Lake Como at Lecco, where we cross the river Adda to explore the Triangolo Lariano, the high area of land that separates the two arms of the lake. The Romans called the lake 'Lucius Larianus', and the derivation 'Lario' can be found in several village names. The day concludes with a visit to Bellagio, one of the most beautifully sited resorts in Europe. It is set in a sheltered spot on the point of the Triangle, which is aptly called Punta Spartivento — the 'Point that Divides the Wind'.

From **Menaggio**★ (*i*✝⛰▲△✕⛽⊕WC; Walks 12,13) take the car ferry to Varenna. It is only a short crossing but, just like any trip on the lake, it is a delightful experience. Varenna is a medieval town of Roman origin. It has a pretty square, narrow cobbled streets and a tiny harbour, as well as two notable villas. Villa Cipressi has beautiful terraced gardens, whilst Villa Monastero, which was built for Cistercian nuns in the 13th century, is now a science centre with a wonderful outlook over the lake.

From the ferry terminal in **Varenna**★ (*i*✝♜⛰▲✕⛽**M**WC; Walk 19) drive to the main road where you turn left and then immediately right, signposted to PERLEDO/ESINO. Go under the railway bridge and up through the hairpin bends, with high cliffs towering above. Continue through **Perledo**, enjoying the incredible views over **Lake Como**, but taking care on the narrow road. You climb again after the village, to come to a beautiful viewpoint (📷). There follows a most scenic drive as you wind up the north side of the steep **Esino Valley**.

The road angle eases as you come to **Esino Lario** (13.5km **M**), sometimes referred to as the 'Pearl of Grigna', with the church perched on a knoll above its many fine villas. Here also is the Grigna Museum, with a history of the mountain and interesting geological and fossil specimens.

The tour now follows signs for CAINALO, then leaves the Cainalo road off to the right and heads left for VALSASSINA on a quiet road, soon passing the turning for Walk 20 and Picnic 9. Opposite a little chapel you can look down to Dervio across flower-strewn meadows. Further on there is a tiny viewpoint and layby (📷) with fine views of Grigna and across Bellagio to the western shores of Lake Como. Luckily this route has several more laybys, so the wonderful landscape can be enjoyed to the full.

The road drops down through **Parlasco**, which has a large white church. The many little villages dotting the hillside across the valley make this a very attractive scene. Continue winding your way down into **Valsassina**, to come to

Bellagio, with a ferry at the waterfront

the ancient, but now rather industrial town of **Cortenova** (30km). At the main road, turn right and follow the valley under the impressive crags of the Grigna massif, passing through **Primaluna** (33.5km **M**), once the 'capital' of Valsassina and now home to the 'Museum of the Valley'.

Entering **Introbio** (37km ✕⛽ ⊕**M**), all traffic is directed round to the right. But just metres past that sign, on the far side of the zebra crossing, turn 90° left (where a small sign on the wall indicates 'CASCATA'). The track to the **Cascata de Troggia**, a beautiful waterfall, is on the far side of the motor museum — the second large grey building on the left. Park nearby and take a short walk (30 minutes return) to see this graceful fall, which drops into an emerald pool and was once visited by Leonardo da Vinci.

Then drive back to the one-way system and carry on up the valley, noting the huge statue of the Madonna beside the road as you go through **Pasturo** (♜). Continue past the turning for Barzio/Cremeno, two attractive villages facing the more benign eastern slopes of Grigna, and with the ski centre of Piani di Bobbio on the mountain behind. The road now climbs to the **Colle di Balisio**. Cross the col and start the descent into Lecco.

Go straight over the roundabout in **Ballabio** (46.5km ⛽).* Easy bends lead to the unsigned village of **Laorca** (50.5km; Walk 21), where the road is busy and narrow. (It's also likely to be slow-going through Lecco.) Beyond Laorca, at the first set of traffic lights (beside an Erg petrol station), turn left at the elongated roundabout, following signs for COMO. Keep straight on to the next roundabout, where you turn right. (But for Walk 22 or Picnic 10, turn left here, then take the first right on VIA AI POGGI, signed for the FUNIVIA.) Continue downhill to a large, double roundabout, where you go left and then immediately right (again for COMO). Keep ahead under a railway bridge and then, at a roundabout, go straight on to cross the **river Adda** on an old bridge dating from 1336. **Lecco** (54.5km ***i*** ▲▲△✕

---

*But if you are not going to Walk 22 or Picnic 10, you could take the third exit from the roundabout — going through some tunnels and avoiding the congestion in Lecco. Then rejoin the tour at the 00km-point.

⛽⊕MWC) is the second largest town on Lake Como. From its beginnings as a fishing village in a picturesque setting, it has become a very modern, industrialised town but still retains some lovely old buildings.

On the far side of the river Adda turn right for COMO. At the roundabout by another bridge, turn left for MILANO, ignoring the signposts straight on to Como and Bellagio. Continue on a dual carriageway, passing **Lago di Annone** on your left. Now follow signs for COMO/ERBA to reach **Suello**. Beyond **Pusiano** (66km), turn right at traffic lights, signed to BELLAGIO/CANZO (among others). The road climbs and you quickly reach **Lago del Segrino**, where you follow signs for CANZO. At the far end of the lake you can park and take a brisk walk on the popular fitness circuit (Picnic 11). Continue through **Canzo** (73km ✕⛽), a town geared up for sports enthusiasts, towards ASSO and BELLAGIO. Keep on the main road through **Asso** (74.5km), ignoring a right turn for Bellagio, and then keep left towards BELLAGIO and SORMANO, to go through a short tunnel. You are now back in rural countryside with villages clustered on the hillsides.

Turn left for SORMANO, climbing on a good road and then take a sharp turn right to zigzag up more steeply, with excellent views across the tree-lined hills. You drive along a quiet road — a pleasant change from the metropolis of Lecco! Be careful through the narrow streets of **Sormano** (80km ✝), which has an attractive church, and then turn right for PIAN DEL TIVANO to continue up through woodland. Watch out for more fitness enthusiasts, who may be training on this road as far as the shoulder of a ridge at **Colma** (85km ✕📷; Walk 23; Picnic 12). Here there is ample parking, a small observatory and wonderful views.

The road now descends beneath the grassy southern slopes of Monte San Primo (Walk 24) to reach the **Piano del Tivano**, a flat grassland area, popular with horse riders. Carry on through the high village of **Zelbio** and past the houses of **Veleso**, terraced on the hillside. Cross the river and immediately keep left for NESSO. You now drop very steeply but with spectacular views across Lake Como as you descend.

Take care at the very sharp right turn to Bellagio when you meet the main road in **Nesso** (98.5km). This ancient village still has a section of its old wall, and an attractive gorge just where the **Torrente Nesso** enters the lake. The lakeside drive that follows is comparatively quiet — through **Lezzeno** (✝), passing an attractive frescoed church and, as you go through the pretty village of **Sostra**, there are some lovely views across to Lenno.

Leaving the built-up area, continue beside the lake, looking out for the parking spot on the left (📷), just after a bridge, to enjoy more wonderful views. Soon you enter **Bellagio**★ (112km *i*⛪▲✕⛽⊕M❀WC), passing villas Trotti and Melzi, the latter noted for its spring gardens of rhododendrons and azaleas. Carry on to the waterfront and ferry terminal, just before the old town centre. Do explore Bellagio, 'the Pearl of Lario'; a climb up the famous steps of Salita Serbelloni should be on the list of every visitor.

The final stage of the tour is by ferry again, and here you have a choice — the direct one to **Menaggio** or, if it is more convenient, the ferry to Cadenabbia (about 3km south of Menaggio).

Car tour 5, *Garda*: A TOUR OF FOUR LAKES

Riva del Garda • Limone sul Garda • Voltino • Vesio • Tignale • Gargnano • Navazzo • Valvestino • Persone • Moerna • Capovalle • Lemprato • Pieve Vecchia • Ponte Caffaro • Storo • Bezzecca • Pieve di Ledro • Molina di Ledro • Biacesa • Riva del Garda

144.5km/90mi; 3.5-4 hours' driving

On route: Picnics 13, (14, 15), 16, 17, 18, 19, 20, (21); Walks 25, (26, 27, 28, 29), 30, 31, 32, 33, 34, (35), 36, 37, 38

With steep cliffs that drop straight to its shores, the north of Lake Garda was little known to tourists until the construction of the lakeside roads. The 'Gardesana Occidentale' (the western shore road) opened in 1932. This amazing highway, which we use for short stretches on our tour, cuts through the cliffs creating numerous tunnels. The countryside to the northwest of the lake is both varied and spectacular, providing a very stimulating drive with plenty of opportunities for short walks, picnics and visits to places of interest.

Leave **Riva del Garda★** (*i*▮▲▲▲ Δ✕⛽⊕MWC; Walk 25; Picnic 13) following signs for LIMONE SUL GARDA and quickly pass through a modern tunnel. Drive through a series of older tunnels to reach the Hotel Splendid Palace, where there is indeed a splendid view down to **Limone sul Garda★** (10.5km *i*▲▲▲Δ✕⛽⊕WC; Walk 30). The main lakeside road runs above the old town, now pedestrianised. This popular resort, most likely named after the lemon tree, is busy and almost completely given over to tourism, but it is still delightful. The narrow streets, full of flower-bedecked houses clustered around the small harbour, retain much of their original charm.

Opposite some tennis courts, look out for the right turn to TREMOSINE that takes you up by terraces of olive trees and through the hillside village of **Voltino** (16.5km *i*▲▲▲✕), where a right turn leads to Walk 31 and Picnic 16. Continue to **Vesio** (19km ▲▲✕⛽⛩ 📷), with fine views over the fertile terraces of the **Tremosine plateau**. On the edge of this village turn right for TIGNALE (but take the *next* turn right for Walk 32). The road rises past Vesio's fine church into the attractive centre, where the road is narrow. There is a car park beyond the cobbled section.

Leave Vesio following signs for TIGNALE, to drive through woods and then green meadows (this district is renowned for its butter and cheese production), before dropping down into a deep gorge. The scenery is quite dramatic as you make your way towards Prabione, which you bypass, before coming to a small col below Monte Castello (Walk 33, Picnic 17).

Continue along a wider road through **Tignale** (32km ✕) and down the zigzags, with some great viewpoints (📷 with parking) over **Lake Garda**. At one point the road crosses a precipitous cliff face; watch out here for fallen stones, especially after heavy rain. You then go by more olive terraces before rejoining the main road along the lakeside, where the tour turns right. Immediately enter a tunnel that, at its exit, neatly frames the hill of Monte Castello di Gaino (Walk 34). At the 16th-century town of **Gargnano★** (43km *i*▲▲▲✕⛽⊕M), with its distinctive onion-domed church and ancient Franciscan monastery, there are tiers of terraced citrus orchards and, by the lakeside, the locals sell delicious oranges and lemons. Turn right before the centre towards COSTA/VALVESTINO. Climb up the wooded hillside, where there are large houses amidst lombardy pines and, higher up, fine views to Monte Castello di Gaino.

Keep following signs for VALVESTINO and go through **Navazzo** (51.5km ✕; Walk 34) heading towards the huge bulk of Monte Pizzocolo. The countryside now becomes much wilder and more remote, with the road narrow and convoluted as you drive alongside the edge of a deep gorge. You pass the dam for the **Lago di Valvestino** — a reservoir created for hydroelectric power in 1960, flooding the **Valvestino Valley** — and follow the banks, bridging two of its side valleys along the way. There are plenty of spots to park, especially near the far end of the lake. What a peaceful place, with no human habitation to spoil the solitude! After driving through a short tunnel you reach a few houses and a bar-*osteria*.

At the next junction turn right towards TURANO/MAGASA, following the river up the narrow valley between limestone cliffs. Just before you come to a roundabout (66.5km), where you keep left, the village of Turano is visible on the hillside above. (For Walk 35 turn right here towards MAGASA/CIMA REST). You now begin a long climb, passing the turn for Turano, up to **Persone** (✕), a traditional hill village, which has an information board in English beside the car park on the far side. The road continues up through trees to **Moerna** (72.5km ⛪ 🛆 📷; Walk 36, Picnic 18), where there is another information board and parking just below the small cemetery. This is an enchanting village — a cluster of houses in a magnificent setting high in the valley.

From Moerna continue on the winding road, but now downhill, to the larger and more scattered village of **Capovalle** (77km ✕). Well over 1km outside the village, turn right for IDRO, joining a wide road that snakes down to the lake. Just after a short tunnel, look out for an excellent viewpoint (📷) over **Lake Idro** and to the mountains beyond. Drive through **Crone**, following signs for BRESCIA/TRENTO, to pass the inviting beaches of **Lemprato** (90km ✕🛆; Picnic 19) at the southern end of the lake. Lake Idro is much smaller and quieter than Lake Garda, but the mountains still rise steeply from its shores. It is the highest lake in Lombardy, over 360m/1200ft above sea level and, in some parts it is over 300m/1000ft deep. You cross a small bridge to reach a T-junction in **Pieve Vecchia**

Lake Idro from Lemprato (Picnic 19)

View over Alveo Lago Bondo (Walk 32)

(92km *i*✕⛽), where you turn right towards TRENTO. The road runs above the lakeshore, giving good views across to the far side. Go through **Anfo** before reaching the large town of **Ponte Caffaro** (105.5km *i*■✕⛽⊕).

Immediately after crossing a bridge over the **river Caffaro** turn right, signposted to BONDONE, to drive through a flat cultivated area. You cross the **river Chiese** and then turn left for Storo. Enjoy this flat, straight road past attractive farms. In **Storo** (111.5km ⊕) follow signs for RIVA and, once you have crossed the river, start to zigzag steeply up the dramatic and narrow **Valle d'Ampola**. You cross the **river Palvico** (📷), beside an attractive and unusual waterfall — the water cascades down a protruding rock.

After the steep climb there is a large parking area just before the **Passo d'Ampola**. What a sharp contrast in the scenery! Gone is the steep-sided, rocky ravine, replaced instead by a wide, green fertile valley. Drive through **Tiarno** (✝), which has a pretty church in a lovely rural setting, before coming to **Tiarno de Sotto**, another scenic village.

The road now drops to **Bezzecca** (128km *i*✕), an attractive town, before continuing on to **Pieve di Ledro**★ (129.5km *i*▲△✕⛽WC; Picnic 20), a small but busy tourist resort on the shores of **Lake Ledro**. (You could turn right here to park and walk along a lakeside footpath which starts near the Hotel Lido and runs to Mezzolago.) You enjoy lovely open views as you drive along the 3km-long lakeside road (⛩), passing through **Mezzolago**. Beyond the end of the lake you come to the narrow streets of **Molina di Ledro**★ (134km *i*△✕**M**). The remains of many ancient lake dwellings have been found in Lake Ledro, and there is a reconstruction of one here, as well as a small museum. Continue down the road, overlooking the attractive rooftops of Pre, with little vineyards on the hillsides, to reach the quiet old village of **Biacesa** (137.5km; Walks 37, 38). (Just beyond is the turn to Pregasina, a cliff-girt village overlooking the northern end of Lake Garda; Picnic 21). You now drive through two long tunnels to emerge on to the open hillside above the fertile plain to the north of Lake Garda. Follow the road down to a T-junction, where a right turn will take you back to **Riva del Garda** (144.5km).

Walking

Nearly everyone who visits the Italian Lakes will do some walking, be it a stroll through the narrow streets of the fascinating lakeside towns or along the waterfront promenades. But for more serious walkers the mountains beckon, with many exciting and varied opportunities. There are remote villages, isolated churches and wonderful viewpoints to visit in the encircling hills. Walk through old olive terraces, in peaceful woodlands or along high-level ridges to reach dramatic peaks. History will come alive when you discover reminders of wartime conflict, and the many shrines which line the ancient paths and mule-tracks emphasise the importance that religion played in the lives of local people. Although strong legs are needed for many of the climbs, we have included plenty of walks for *everyone* to enjoy and, on some routes, we drive to high-level starting points or use a cable car for easy access to the mountaintops.

Grading, waymarking, maps, GPS

We hope everyone who uses this guide will find plenty of walks to suit his/her ability. We have assigned them **grades** according to distance covered, height climbed, roughness of paths and any particular difficulties. There is a quick overview of each walk's grade in the Contents, where we've only had space to show the *lowest* grade of a *main* walk: for full details, including shorter or alternative easier versions, see the walk itself. Here is a brief overview of the four gradings:

- ● very easy (perhaps a short climb to a viewpoint); good surfaces underfoot
- ● easy-moderate — ascents/descents of no more than about 300-500m/1000-1800ft; good surfaces underfoot; easily followed
- ● moderate-strenuous — ascents/descents may be over 500m/1800ft; variable surfaces underfoot — you must be sure-footed and agile; possible route-finding problems in poor visibility
- ● expert — only suitable for very experienced hillwalkers with a head for heights and used to constant exposure

Any of the above grades may be followed by:

- ! *possibility* of vertigo — for those with no head for heights at all
- !! *danger* of vertigo — you must have a very good head for heights

Many of Italy's walking routes are **signposted** and/or **waymarked** with red and white flashes. ***Waymarked routes are shown on our maps by an unbroken black line.*** If you deviate from our notes, *for your safety it is essential to stay on these routes.*

You should find the **maps** in this book adequate for all of our walks but, if you wish to go further afield, you should have the relevant sheet map and a compass/gps. Maps are readily available on the ground or can be bought before you travel (see 'Useful contacts', page 29). There is a wide range of maps from which to choose. Most readily available are the Kompass 1:50 000 maps, which clearly show all waymarked paths, but geographical detail is lacking, and the contour interval is 100m. For lakes Maggiore and Orta we recommend the Cartine Zanetti 1:30 000 series. Around Lake Garda, the free Garda Trentino 1:30 000 map (issued by the Garda Trentino tourist offices in Riva del Garda, Torbole and Arco) are most useful. Roads and tracks are being continually upgraded, and you will come across inaccuracies on all the maps, so do use them in conjunction with our notes.

Free **GPS track** downloads and **height profiles** are available for all our walks: see the Italian Lakes page on the Sunflower website. Please bear in mind, however, that GPS readings should *never* be relied upon as your sole reference point, as conditions can change overnight.

The Italian Alpine Club (CAI)

The CAI (Club Alpino Italiano) has over 300,000 members, owning and managing many mountain huts *(rifugi)*, and is responsible for the waymarking of much of the path network throughout Italy. It also maintains an excellent mountain rescue service (see 'Useful contacts', page 29).

Equipment and safety

For each walk we have indicated only *special equipment* necessary, eg map and compass, walking sticks, and if walking shoes will be sufficient. The contents of your rucksack must reflect the weather, the time of year and the length of the walk.

- Always take plenty of food and water.
- Wear good walking boots with ankle support on all walks except those indicated.
- Take adequate clothing. Extra clothing should be included even on a warm day, if tackling a mountain route.
- Take sun protection cream and sunglasses.
- Take a basic first aid kit.

Extra equipment for mountain walks:

- Waterproof/windproof jacket
- Sunhat/warm hat and gloves
- Map, compass, whistle, mobile (the emergency number for the police is 112; to check out local mountain rescue numbers ask at the relevant tourist information office, but remember: mobiles *may* be unreliable in the mountains).

Safety

- Do not overestimate your ability.
- Avoid walking alone; leave word of your intended route.
- Be prepared to turn back if the route proves too difficult.
- Turn back if the weather deteriorates — thunderstorms can develop very quickly, especially in summer.
- Avoid mountain ridge walks if storms are forecast.
- Falling rocks: some mountain paths may be eroded, and on loose surfaces care must be taken — the danger of rock fall being greatest after frost or heavy rainfall. Try to avoid knocking stones off the path as you are walking. If this does happen, *always* shout a warning to those below.
- *Never* tackle a *via ferrata* without proper training and equipment. See www.viaferrata.org for more information.

Weather

The Alps and Dolomites protect the lakes from northern European winters, and the climate can be almost Mediterranean. For walking the most favourable seasons are from April to June and September and October. In spring the air sparkles, and flowers and greenery adorn the hillsides, though snow may linger well into May on the higher summits. The quiet autumn months are wonderful, when the grapes are being harvested and rich colours clothe the countryside. For walkers, we would suggest avoiding July and August, as these are the hottest months and the busiest. Winter will give a different perspective to the area, with snow covering the mountaintops, and anyone heading for the hills at this time must be suitably equipped with ice-axe and crampons. Of the four lakes, Maggiore, Lugano and Como have the lowest rainfall in summer and autumn. Lake Garda's precipitation at this time comes mainly in short thundery downpours. Here winter is the driest period, with many sunny days.

If you are planning a long walk, especially in the mountains, do get a weather forecast — available at hotels and tourist information offices. Water sources in the mountains may be dry in summer, so ***always*** carry an adequate supply.

Where to stay

Accommodation is readily available throughout the Italian Lakes area, and our walks can be reached from many towns. For each walk we have indicated the closest places to stay under 'Nearest accommodation'. The Italian Tourist Board, both in the UK and in the country itself (see 'Useful contacts', page 29) will gladly provide you with information about hotels, hostels and self-catering establishments in all areas. Camping sites are numerous, and the standard is generally excellent. Wild camping is prohibited.

Nuisances

The viper is Italy's only poisonous **snake**. It is shy and can be found mostly in grassy undergrowth and rock crevices. Always wear boots or good shoes and long trousers when walking in areas where they may be present. If bitten, keep the victim calm and bind the affected limb tightly (do not use a tourniquet) before seeking medical help. An antivenom is available from pharmacists.

Italians love **hunting and shooting**. During the season, from October to March, the sound of gunfire may accompany your walks. It is essential to stay on marked paths or tracks (do *not* hide) and, if the hunters are about, make enough noise to ensure that your presence is known or you may be a succulent morsel in the pot as well! You may come across elaborately constructed hides with small caged birds — mostly blackbirds and thrushes hanging on tree branches all around. These attract other small birds, which can then be shot. To many this sport is repugnant. You may also encounter hunters with dogs, but we have always found them respectful and courteous.

Organisation of the walks

All our walks are grouped according to the car tour from which they are accessed. This is clearly shown on the fold-out touring map. Each walk starts from a parking place or from a town centre and, where indicated, can also be reached by public transport. Most of our main walks are circular or linear, while the short walks are often out and back.

At the top of each walk you will find essential information — distance and time, grade, equipment, transport, nearest accommodation and, if applicable, alternatives for shorter or longer walks.

Below is a key to the **symbols** on the walking maps.

motorway	spring, waterfall, etc	specified building
main road	water treatment plant	monument
secondary road	church.chapel	cave.hide
motorable track	shrine or cross	quarry, mine
42 waymarked route/CAI N° *referred to in text*	cemetery	campsite.stadium
track, path, trail	picnic tables	❷ waypoint
268 difficult path	best views	P picnic suggestion (see pages 8-13)
2→ main walk	bus stop	map continuation
2→ alternative walk	car parking	ski or goods lift
park boundary	railway station	cable car
400 height in metres	castle, fort	mountain refuge

Footpath sign (Walk 36). The red and white stripes indicate that all three routes signposted here are waymarked by the CAI (see page 26). Although the signs are in Italian, the meaning is clear: protect flora, do not light open fires, foul water supplies or leave rubbish.

Country code for walkers

- Keep on tracks and paths.
- Heed warning signs.
- Do not pick plants or disturb birds and animals.
- Do not damage alpine huts, signs, or visitors' books.
- Keep dogs under control.
- Do not cause rock falls.
- Keep gates closed.
- Prevent forest fires.
- Take your litter home.
- Make no unnecessary noise.
- Greet other walkers — 'Buongiorno' or 'Ciao' and a smile are sufficient.

Useful contacts

For maps, guides, etc

www.amazon.co.uk — for travel guides, dictionaries and language guides

Stanfords
12-14 Long Acre
Covent Garden
London WC2E 9LP
Tel: 020 7836 1321
Web: www.stanfords.co.uk
E-mail: customer.services @stanfords.co.uk

The Map Shop
15 High Street
Upton upon Severn
Worcs WR8 0HJ
Tel: 01684 593146
Fax: 01684 594559
Web: www.themapshop.co.uk
E-mail: themapshop @btinternet.com

For general information and accommodation details

ENIT (Italian Tourist) Office
1 Princes Street
London W1B 2AY
Tel: 020 7408 1254
Web: www.enit.it
E-Mail: info.london@enit.it

www.illagomaggiore.com/ Specific tourist information for Lake Maggiore

www.visitgarda.com/ Specific tourist information for Lake Garda

www.emmeti.it/index.uk.html Covers the whole of Italy in great detail.

Special interest

The Italian Alpine Club — *Club Alpino Italiano* (CAI)
Via Petrella 19, 20124 Milano
Tel: (00 39) 02 2057231;
Fax: (00 39) 02 205723201
Web: www.cai.it. Go to the link 'Le sezioni del CAI' and select the local club for its e-mail address and other information.

Italian for walkers

Italian is a musical language and, as much of English is derived from Latin, you will find many words easy to understand. Do try to learn a few phrases — it is fun, and your efforts will be greatly appreciated (Italian phrase books are readily available). Around the lakes, German is the most widely spoken foreign language, but English is usually understood. Below we have listed a simple guide to pronunciation and a few basic words and phrases, concentrating on those you may need while walking or touring.

Walk 16: shrine set in a plane tree at the Santuario della Madonna del Soccorso, Ossuccio

pronunciation of vowels

a as in car
e as in met
i as in meet
o as in not
u as in look

pronunciation of consonants

c as in can (but c before e or i is pronounced as in chin)
ch as in can
g as in got (but g before e or i is pronounced as in jot)
gh as in got
gi as in billion
gn as in bunion
h is always silent
r — is always a rolled rrr sound
sc before e or i is pronounced as in shin; before a, h, o or u as in skate
z as in tights

A few useful phrases and words

Hello/Good morning	Ciao/Buongiorno
Goodbye	Arrivederci/Ciao
Please	Per favore
Thank you	Grazie
You're welcome/that's fine	Prego
Yes, No	Si, No
Do you speak English?	Parla *(sing)*; Parli *(pl)* Inglese?
Help!	Aiuto!
Go away!	Vai via!
I'm lost	Mi sono perduto *(m)*; perduta *(f)*
Where is?	Dov'e?
How far/How long?	Quanto distanza/Quanto tempo?
Please write it down	Per favore me lo scriva
I understand/don't understand	Capisco/Non capisco
Go straight ahead	Sempre diritto
Left/Right	Sinistra/Destra
Near/Far	Vicini/Lontano
Early/Late	Presto/Tardi

Easy/Difficult	Facile/Difficile
Upper/Middle/Lower	Superiore/Mezzo/Inferiore
Little/Big	Piccolo/Grande
Open/Closed	Aperto/Chiuso
North/East/South/West	Nord/Est/Sud/Ovest
Northern/Eastern	Settentrione/Orientale
Southern/Western	Meridionale/Occidentale
Toilets	Gabinetti
Restaurant	Ristorante/Trattoria
Ice cream parlour	Gelateria
Hotel/Guest house	Albergo/Pensione
Hostel/Camping	Ostello/Campeggio
Drinking water	Acqua potabile

Below are some other useful words, including those you may see on the maps and in our text.

Italian	*English*	*English*	*Italian*
Bocca	Mouth/Gap	Bridge	Ponte
Bosco	Wood	Castle	Castello
Campo	Field	Cave	Grotto
Cappella	Chapel	Cemetery	Cimitero
Casa	House	Chapel	Cappella
Cascata	Waterfall	Church	Chiesa
Castello	Castle	Cliff	Scogliera
Chiesa	Church	Farm	Fattoria
Cima	Summit	Field	Campo
Cimitero	Cemetery	Fog	Nebbia
Colle	Hill/Pass	Forest	Foresta
Fattoria	Farm	Gardens	Giardini
Fiume/Torrente	River	Harbour	Porto
Foresta	Forest	Hill/Pass	Colle
Giardini	Gardens	House	Casa
Grotto	Cave	Island	Isola
Isola	Island	Lake	Lago
Lago	Lake	Map	Mappa
Mappa	Map	Mountain	Montagna
Montagna	Mountain	Mouth/Gap	Bocca
Nebbia	Fog	Pass	Passo
Neve	Snow	Path	Sentiero
Passo	Pass	Peak	Picco
Picco	Peak	Rain	Ploggia
Ploggia	Rain	River	Fiume/Torrente
Ponte	Bridge	Road/Way	Strada
Porto	Harbour	Street	Via
Scogliera	Cliff	Snow	Neve
Sentiero	Path	Summit	Cima
Sole	Sun	Sun	Sole
Strada	Road/Way	Thunderstorm	Temporale
Temporale	Thunderstorm	Tower	Torre
Torre	Tower	Valley	Valle
Valle	Valley	Wind	Vento
Vento	Wind	Wood	Bosco
Via	Street	Waterfall	Cascata

Walk 1: FROM CHEGLIO TO CANNOBIO VIA MONTE CARZA AND MONTE PIAN BELLO

View north from Monte Carza

Distance/time: 15km/9.3mi; 4h56min
Grade: ● moderate; an easy ascent of 550m/1800ft, followed by a pleasant ridge walk. The return to Cannobio involves nearly 1250m/4100ft of descent.
Equipment: see page 26. Walking poles, swimsuit. Refreshments are available from a bar in Traffiume .

Transport: 🚌 Trarego bus from Cannobio or Cannero Riviera (see 'Transport information' inside the back cover); alight at Cheglio. The walk ends back at Cannobio.
Nearest accommodation: Cannobio or Cannero Riviera
Short walk: Monte Carza. 5km/3mi; 1h40min. ● Easy, with an ascent/descent of 350m/1150ft; equipment as main walk. Access by 🚌 as main walk or 🚗: from Cannobio drive to Cannero Riviera and turn right in the town for Viggiona and Trarego. This initially steep, twisting and narrow road soon improves. Park just outside Cheglio, at the junction for Colle (1.5km/1mi beyond Viggiona; (46° 2.106'N, 8° 40.399'E). Follow the main walk to **Monte Carza** (ⓐ); return the same way.

A short but steep bus journey does much of the ascent for you on this walk. The busy lakeside is left behind and, after climbing through attractive woodlands and past old farms, you can enjoy beautiful and extensive views across to the Alps, along Lake Maggiore and over the Valle Cannobina. After the long descent you reach a picturesque church beside the river — a great place for a refreshing swim.

Start the walk at the road junction at **Cheglio**: walk up the road signposted to COLLE. Just after a sharp S bend, take signposted ROUTE 13, a lane that goes up left towards Monte Carza (**6min**). After only three minutes — just opposite the first of two houses — take a stepped path up to the right (RED/WHITE WAYMARKS). You will see the distinctive peak of Cima di Morissolo on the far side of the Cannero Valley and there are fleeting views down to Lake Maggiore. The good path continues steeply up through woods of birch, chestnut and pine and at one point crosses a bridge above a cascading waterfall. After passing beneath an electricity line the path becomes less distinct and climbs up to a fenced grassy field. Go left, following the fence, and look for a waymark on a telegraph pole ahead. The next pole uphill is in front of some small houses. Here follow waymarks to the right, behind the first house and along to a concrete ramp. Climb this to meet a road (**34min**) and a SIGNPOST FOR ROUTE 13. Cross the road and walk along a grassy track, to reach the ridge at a T-JUNCTION by a group of pine trees (❷; **41min**).

Head right here for Monte Carza, along a grassy path with clear waymarks. At a small COL, where there is a junction of tracks, continue straight on uphill, following the signpost to gain the SUMMIT of **Monte Carza** (a; **54min**). From this peaceful peak the views are wide and include the snowy Alps to the northeast and over Lake Maggiore to the south. Trees obscure the view north from the top, but if you walk to the obvious large metal board you can look over the lower regions of the Valle Cannobina. Just below the summit is a superbly built stone MEMORIAL and SHRINE.

From the summit retrace your steps to the junction at the 41min-point (2; **1h13min**). About 10 metres beyond the track that goes off right, look for a narrow path that heads uphill into the trees. You will first be in woods and later at their edge, as you rise past a number of summits, the first of which is **Cima Ologno** (b). Continue westward along Ologno's southern flanks; some 15 minutes from the T-junction you leave the trees and the path widens out, then plunges back into the woods. There's a stone-built marker at the TOP of **Monte Pian Bello** (c; **2h**) — but no views; it's unfortunately smothered in thick trees.

Descend quickly to a tree-covered COL and then climb again to **Cima Forcola** (d; **2h14min**). Breaks in the trees allow some views over the lake and the Cannero Valley. Descend again, noticing the military trenches just before you reach a signposted col, **Boccetta Tondone** (3; **2h26min**). Continue along the ridge on a fainter, unmarked path to the SUMMIT of **Cima Tondone** (a; **2h41min**), which offers superb views to the west over the upper reaches of the Valle Cannobina, where small farm buildings dot the hillside. With the Alps beyond, this is a wonderful lunch spot!

Retrace your steps to **Boccetta Tondone** (3) and turn left for SOMMALEMNA. The clearly waymarked path descends through the trees for about 15 minutes to the edge of some old pasture at the ruined alm of **Sommalemna** (4), from where there are fine views across to Monte Limidario. Continue for another three minutes, to arrive at a junction beside a ruined building (**3h 07min**). Follow the signpost to the right for TRAFFIUME, crossing two small streams and, soon after, easily ford a fast flowing, larger stream. In another five minutes you reach a semi-ruined building with an empty (unfortunately!) wine keg in the doorway. Turn left here, following the waymarks, on a rough path down past a house and through a cleared area to reach the end of a MOTORABLE TRACK (**3h30min**). Turn right, now on a rough track, following faint waymarks that lead past another building and a water trough beside a field. At first keep to the edge of this field, around to the right, and then follow a small stream down to a rough track. Cross this (*do not* cross the old wooden bridge) and follow the stream again, crossing it after about 50m. Seek out more waymarks that lead down to two small wooden bridges and walk beside a high wire fence to reach a signpost in **Pianoni** (5; **3h39min**).

Follow the sign for TRAFFIUME past a house (the waymarks here are clear but widely spaced). In two minutes cross a stream and, keeping to the left of another house, join an old cobbled way. This path zigzags steeply downhill, passing a SHRINE from where there is a good view across Traffiume and Cannobio. Five minutes after the next SHRINE you come to the main valley road beside a waterfall. Cross this road to rejoin the cobbles that quickly lead to another road. Turn left and walk downhill to the beautifully situated church of **Santa Anna** (**4h23min**; Picnic 1) that stands at the end of the impressive gorge, the **Orrido da Santa Anna** (6), which you can see from the rear of the church (there is a toilet here). This narrow gorge is popular with scuba divers and is crossed by a wonderful old stone BRIDGE. A stony riverside beach, an attractive and popular suntrap, is gained by descending the wide steps on the far side of the road bridge and has lovely deep pools for swimming.

Continue along the road to a 16th-century chapel at the edge of **Traffiume**. Leave the main village road here and continue *straight on* along VIA TORRI, which becomes narrow and eventually cobbled. When you reach an asphalt road, turn left and, ignoring three further turns to the left, reach a T-junction. Turn left to come to a ROUNDABOUT opposite the church of **Santa Maria Turificata** (7; **4h32min**).

Turn right at the roundabout, after 70m passing a FOUNTAIN with a stone man spouting water from his mouth. Keep left at the next junction and then turn left beside a very large COVERED SHRINE (8). Walk past commercial buildings before the road drops to a junction. Turn right along CASALI MASSERECCI. You now walk between attractive houses and well-kept gardens. At a sharp left-hand bend, bear right to cross the **Torrente Cannobino** on a suspension bridge. At the far side, turn right on VIA SAN ROCCO. Follow this to a junction with two left turns. Take the second left and walk along beside a garage on VIA ANTONIO GIOVANOLA, a pretty street with interesting shops. Follow this road to the end of your walk at the CAMPANILE in **Cannobio** (9; **4h56min**).

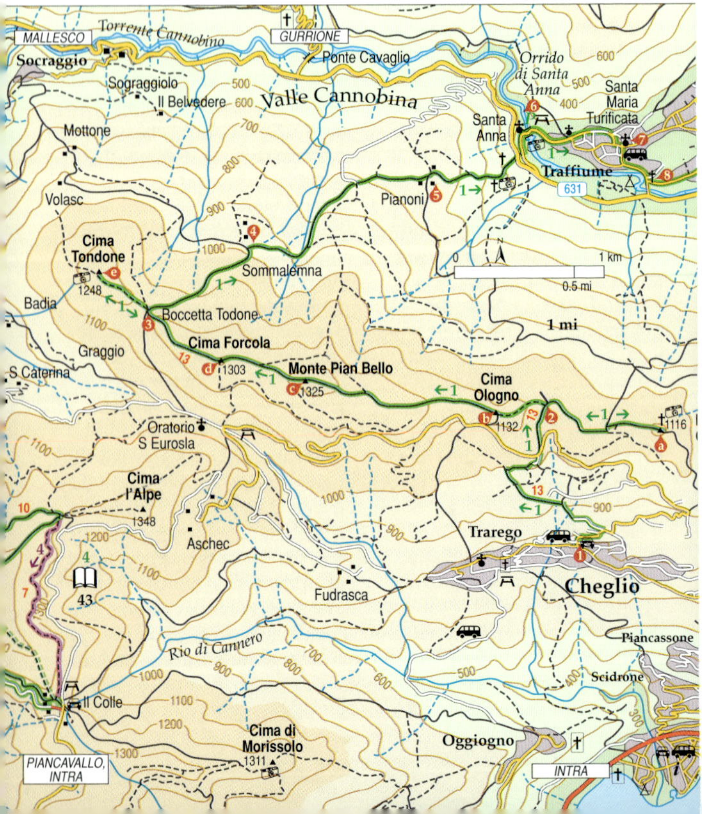

See also photograph page 13
Distance: 7.5km/4.7mi; 2h25min
Grade: ● easy-moderate; with about 300m/1000ft of ascent. Mainly on clear, waymarked woodland paths and tracks
Equipment: see page 26. Refreshments available at start and end
Transport: 🚌 or ⛴ to Cannero Riviera (or Cannobio)*; see 'Transport information' inside the back cover.
Nearest accommodation: Cannobio or Cannero Riviera

Short walks

1 From Cannero Riviera to Carmine Superiore and Carmine Inferiore. 4.5km/2.8mi; 1h14min. ● Easy; equipment and access as above. Follow the main walk to the 1h02min-point (4), then bear right to follow the clear path down to the BUS STOP (b) in **Carmine Inferiore** (same bus as main walk).

2 Carmine Superiore from Carmine Inferiore. 1km/0.6mi; 25-30min. ● Easy. Access: 🚗 or 🚌 (as main walk) to Carmine Inferiore (46° 2.271'N, 8° 42.439'E). *From the car park* (a) walk 175m along the road towards Cannobio and then climb the steps of the signposted path, before turning right to a shrine. *From the bus stop* (b) climb the steps and follow the path to a shrine. *From the shrine* follow the waymarked path that zigzags uphill to meet the main walk at the 1h02min-point (4). Keep left and left again by the first houses, to the church at **Carmine Superiore**. Return the same way.

Enjoying the scenic ferry ride between the attractive lakeside towns of Cannobio and Cannero Riviera is a great way to start the day. On this walk you can look down over the island castles and explore a hillside village that belongs to another age. There are fine viewpoints as you hike through the shady woodlands, making this an ideal short outing when the weather is hot.

Starting from the FERRY TERMINAL in **Cannero Riviera** (1), walk in an easterly direction to the end of the promenade and turn left up narrow VIA MASSIMO AZLEGO. Almost immediately turn right under an archway along VIA ALLE VIGNE to Cannero's old fishing port. Take the cobbled, stepped path between houses No. 6 and 7 and then turn right at the top. Follow this walkway, enjoying unrivalled views over Cannero Riviera, to meet the main road.

*To do the walk in reverse from Cannobio, see notes at the bottom of page 37.

Turn right and then cross on the pedestrian crossing to find the start of the signposted and waymarked path. This path quickly becomes cobbled and rises above the road, to continue on a gentler incline through terraces with fine views of Lake Maggiore. Soon you reach a signposted junction in the semi-ruined hamlet of **Cheggio** (❷; **23min**).

Following the sign for CARMINE SUPERIORE and the waymarks, you begin to descend gently through woodland, to an open area before a large house. From here there is a good view of the two Cannero Castles, each on an island and once connected by a drawbridge (see page 12 for more details).

Continue on the old cobbled path to reach the next junction (**45min**).

Here keep to the left and, after eight minutes, pass an attractive waterfall. Just before you reach the ancient village, you have a fine view of the church through the trees. Walk over a BRIDGE and, turning right, enter **Carmine Superiore** (❸). At the first junction keep right and, at the second, *ignore* the waymarks and keep right again. Continue along the narrow street to the 13th century **Church of San Gottardo** (**1h**; Picnic 2), which is on a rocky promontory overlooking the lake and has marvellous views. The table and benches outside make this a perfect place for a break and a picnic. Inside are paintings and frescoes dating from the 15th and 16th centuries; they were being painstakingly restored when we first walked here many years ago. The whole hamlet — its houses packed close together with their heavy stone roofs and only accessible by old mule tracks — is fascinating and appealing, a microcosm of a bygone age.

To continue, go through the short covered way at the west end of the church (there is a large window here where you can see some of

View across Lake Maggiore to Maccagno from the fascinating village of Carmine Superiore (Picnic 2)

the interior). This walkway leads to a path that descends to meet the waymarked route again. Turn right to quickly come to another junction (❹; **1h02min**). Keep left, following the signpost to MOLINEGGI. In six minutes you reach the end of a road by a big house with a lovely garden. Continue up the steps on the left and walk behind the modern houses of **Carmine Inferiore** (❺). The path — a little rough in places — rises steeply and goes by an attractive little waterfall in about 20 minutes. Climb again to a signposted junction, where you turn right, down a wide cobbled path.

Soon you cross a BRIDGE and enter the semi-ruined hamlet of **Molineggi** (❻; **1h39min**), once a thriving community of millers. The millstones incorporated into the large renovated building here, and the artwork, give clues to the hamlet's past history. Look out for the tiny CHAPEL on the right and continue along the now-wide track that improves and becomes motorable lower down. After about 12 minutes waymarks indicate a path off to the right — a short cut. Cross a stream to quickly join an asphalt road; turn right and walk downhill to the first HAIRPIN BEND, where you turn left along a track (❼; **1h58min**).

Follow this through an open grassy area and past the renovated buildings of **Solivo** (❽), to come to a paved ramp. Near the bottom of this, go along the path to the left; it will take you to the outskirts of Cannobio. The path becomes a narrow asphalt road and reaches a signposted junction where you bear right and and after 75 metres descend to another junction. Turn right here to come quickly to the main road. Go straight across and head down a road signed with a white one-way arrow, and ignore the road to the right. The asphalt turns to cobbles and leads to a small square where there is an ivy-covered SHRINE behind you on the left. Keep right here, past building No. 9, to join VIA ANTONIO GIOVANOLA, where you turn right to end your walk at the CAMPANILE near the main road through **Cannobio** (❾; **2h25min**).

Note: To do this walk in reverse, start from the CAMPANILE in **Cannobio** (❾) and walk down VIA ANTONIO GIOVANOLA. Opposite No. 48 turn left along VIA ROMA and keep left through the little square, beside the ivy-covered SHRINE. Walk along VIA ALLA CAMPAGNA to reach the main road; cross it and, after 70m, turn left to walk up to a signposted junction. Turn left here to follow signs and waymarks to **Cannero Riviera**.

Walk 3: VALLE CANNOBINA CIRCUIT FROM FALMENTA

Distance/time: 14km/8.7mi; 6h
Grade: ● strenuous; mainly on cobbled paths with several steep climbs and descents. Overall ascent/descent 1075m/3527ft. Well waymarked and signposted
Equipment: see page 26. Walking poles. Refreshments are available in Gurro and Falmenta.
Transport: 🚗 Follow signs for Falmenta from Cannobio and park in the village car park (46° 4.307'N, 8° 35.338'E). 🚌 from Cannobio to Falmenta (very limited service; see 'Transport information' inside the back cover).
Nearest accommodation: Cannobio or Cannero Riviera

Shorter walks

1 From Spoccia to Falmenta. 12km/7.4mi; 4h12min. ● Moderate, with 700m/2297ft of ascent and 850m/2790ft of descent. Equipment as above. Access by 🚌 from Cannobio to Spoccia; return by 🚌 from Falmenta. Start by walking up the ramp behind the car park and bus stop, into **Spoccia** village (❸). Follow the narrow street until you reach a small square where you turn left down steps, passing the church. Beside a war memorial, take more steps, heading steeply down below the village and into the trees. At a junction between two shrines, turn right to meet a road. Now follow the main walk from the 1h39min-point (ⓑ) to the end at **Falmenta** (❶).

2 From Spoccia to Cursolo and back. 9km/5.6mi; 3h22min. ● Fairly easy, with 550m/1804ft of ascent. Equipment as main walk. Access by 🚗 as for the main walk but, instead of turning left for Falmenta, continue up the Valle Cannobina, over the bridge at Ponte Spoccia, and then turn right up the steep, narrow road to the car park in **Spoccia** (❸) (46° 5.483'N, 8° 36.194'E). Access by 🚌 as for the Shorter walk (but you must walk quickly to catch the return bus! — keep a careful eye on the time, or perhaps just walk as far as Orasso). Follow ***Shorter walk 1*** described above, but stop at **Cursolo** (❻), exploring the village beyond the old chapel where the main walk turns back. Then retrace your steps to Spoccia.

Old trails are followed on this walk, taking you to several wonderfully scenic hill villages above the Valle Cannobina. Each village retains its individuality, but in each you will see a large church with a separate campanile standing guard over the tightly clustered houses. There is a mixture of old and new, but the air of peaceful permanence will make this a truly memorable outing.

Starting from the CAR PARK in **Falmenta** (❶), walk up the road and around a right-hand bend — to the end of the road. (There is a car park here, too, but parking is limited to two hours.) Continue straight ahead past the BUS STOP (ⓐ), and walk down the narrow cobbled village street, which leads under balconies and an archway to the church of **San Lorenzo**. From the rear of the church continue along the path, following white arrows (you will often see white arrows on this walk). You quickly pass a signpost and then the WASHHOUSE. At the signposted junction below, keep left on the upper path to SPOCCIA. This path enters woods and is at first level and wide. Soon you will see the houses of La Valle ahead, and high above on the other side of the valley is Spoccia. Cross a BRIDGE

(**20min**) and enter **La Valle**. Keep right at the junction, following the sign to SOLGIA.

Leaving La Valle the path drops steeply down to **Solgia**, a charming village, with no car access, where time has stood still. The white arrows lead past a little CHAPEL — you can peep through the windows to see the well-kept interior. The descent from here is steep and ends, after a series of stone-built zigzags, on the main valley road. Turn left to the bridge that spans the **Torrente Cannobino** as it descends through an impressive gorge at **Ponte Spoccia** (❷; **44min**).

Just past the large INFORMATION BOARDS in the village, and by the KM11 MARKER, a signpost on the right-hand side of the road indicates your onward path to SPOCCIA. This steep path passes a SHRINE in 10 minutes and continues spiralling upwards, to reach a road just above a HELICOPTER PAD (ⓑ; **1h39min**). Turn right up this road but, almost immediately, turn left on a well-waymarked path. At a junction between TWO SHRINES turn left to climb the steep steps into the village of **Spoccia** (❸; **1h48min**). The views from the terrace outside the church include your next objectives, Orasso and Cursolo.

Having explored this fascinating village, return to the road that you crossed at the 1h39min-point above ⓑ. Turn right and, after passing several telphers (goods hoists), and just before a left-hand hairpin bend, take the waymarked steps to the right — a WHITE ARROW and 'ORASSO' are painted on the wall at the right. You quickly go by a SHRINE on the right and then continue down the wooded path. The river bubbles below, and the impressive rocky ridge of Rocce del Gridone can be seen through breaks in the trees above. You cross an old stone BRIDGE over a small river flowing through a gorge, after which you begin the ascent to Orasso. About 10 minutes from the bridge there is a good view of Monte Riga, which this walk circumnavigates. Enter **Orasso,** a tranquil, pretty village, and take a break in the shaded grounds surrounding **San Materno** (❹; **2h52min**). On the yellow building beside this church

View to Orasso and Cursolo from the church at Spoccia (top); Oratorio del Sasso at Orasso (left)

is an attractive painting of the Madonna and Child and, on the tall adjoining campanile, a large painted sundial. The church bells in the valley sound the hour twice, with a minute's interval between, and chime once on the half-hour. As the clocks are not synchronised, there is an attractive bell-ringing session every 30 minutes!

From the church continue along VIA ALLE CHIESA. This leads through a passageway with a painted Madonna on the wall and then under an old balcony, which almost roofs the street. After this the narrow street winds to the right and, at the T-junction, you turn left and then almost immediately right (where there is a sign on the wall to CURSOLO). Go up the steps, turn left at the top, and follow the waymarks and white arrows through the village. At a junction beside a water point, go left (clearly signposted to CURSOLO). Walk out of the village and up to the 14th-century **Oratorio del Sasso** (5; **3h 01min**). A bench affords a good opportunity to sit and enjoy the view. In most of these mountain villages many of the houses have been renovated or rebuilt, but there are some that still have their amazingly heavy and beautiful stone roofs.

The walk continues on an easy path with open views across the valley to Gurro. You soon pass some stone-built pools that were once used in the production of hemp. Eventually you cross a BRIDGE over a small stream beside which is a building — possibly an old MILL (C)— and continue up towards Cursolo. In less than one minute you come to a signpost and a path off to the left, which is your onward route. However, we suggest that you go on the short distance to the small old chapel, **Cappella di Cursolo** (⑥; **3h 29min**), which forms a covered way over the path at the entrance to the village. It is worth exploring **Cursolo**, a quiet, peaceful place that is full of interest, and you can also refill your water bottles here. *(Shorter walk 2 returns to Spoccia from this village.)*

Return to the signposted junction below the chapel and turn right for GURRO. After about 12 minutes downhill you reach the main valley road at **Airetta**. Turn right here and walk along the road to the KM16 MARKER. Here take a path on the left, through a break in the road barrier, descending very steeply down to a bridge, the **Ponte Teia**, which crosses high above the **Torrente Cannobino** (⑦; **4h04min**). There is an INFORMATION BOARD here with explanations about the former timber industry in the valley.

From this point it is all uphill to Gurro, and the climb is as hard as the previous descent. Along the way you come to a group of ruined buildings and cross a BRIDGE before continuing up beside a small stream. (Look out for the paintings of the Madonna that still decorate many of the old buildings). At the top of a short flight of steps you meet a T-junction, where you turn right into a grassy area beside some farm buildings. Beyond the clearing, walk up into the village of **Gurro**. Cross the asphalt road and go up the wide path to meet the main village road again, where you turn left uphill to a BAR (⑧; **4h43min**). Opposite are the church, campanile and central square where there is a small museum. There is also a bus stop here. Gurro is a large village boasting modern amenities, a school, an ambulance station and a pharmacy, but the old Italian lifestyle is still much in evidence. The men congregate around the bars while the women, some still in the traditional dress, get on with the work!

Two narrow cobbled streets lead away from the CHURCH. Take the upper one and soon meet a fork where you keep left on the signposted path to FALMENTA. Leave the village under the covered way of another small CHAPEL and then cross an old BRIDGE above a bubbling stream. Continue uphill, following waymarks, to the grassy col of **Mergugna** (⑨; **5h14min**).

Mergugna is just a scattering of houses in a summer grazing area. It has superb views over Gurro and back to Cursolo and a welcome water point. Cross the col, following the sign to FALMENTA, and take a narrow path that starts a few metres in front of a CHAPEL. Now drop steeply, passing another information board about the transhumance (*l'Alpicazione* in Italian), to reach a junction. Turn left here and continue the descent to Falmenta. The angle is now less steep, making for easier walking. As you enter **Falmenta** you can look down on the rooftops, a mixture of old and new houses. Descend a few steps to the church, which has a wonderful stone roof, and reach the little square where there are good views down the Valle Cannobina. Here there is a public toilet and a bar. From the square retrace your steps down VIA ROMA, through Falmenta, to the BUS STOP and CAR PARK (①; **6h**).

Walk 4: MONTE SPALAVERA CIRCUIT

Distance/time: 10.8km/6.7mi; 2h47min
Grade: ● easy; mainly on good paths and tracks, with 375m/ 1230ft of ascent/descent
Equipment: see page 26. No refreshments en route
Transport: Either follow Car Tour 1 to Piancavallo or, for a more direct and easier route, in Intra turn *right* at the fifth roundabout (where the main tour heads left for Miazzina). Parking for Picnic 3 is opposite the T-junction just before Piancavallo). Drive past the Instituto Auxologico and hospital and continue for another 5km/3mi to park at Il Colle (46° 1.477'N, 8° 37.558'E). from Intra in Verbania to the hospital at Piancavallo (limited service; see 'Transport information' inside the back cover); an early start is required to allow sufficient time to complete the walk and catch a return bus. From the hospital you then have a 2.5km/1.6mi walk along the road to Il Colle.
Nearest accommodation: any of the lakeside towns on the western shore of Lake Maggiore
Short walk: Monte Spalavera. 5km/3mi; 1h52min. ● Grade, equipment and access as main walk. Follow the main walk to the SUMMIT of **Monte Spalavera** (❷) and return the same way.

This short easy walk follows in the footsteps of WWI soldiers. From the old mule track you climb up through their old trenches to reach the summit of Monte Spalavera and reap your reward — a spectacular mountain panorama. The return is a gentle stroll through quiet woodlands and then along an open sunny hillside above Valle Intrasca.

This walk starts at the CAR PARK at **Il Colle** (❶). Go up the steps behind the small orange-coloured building and turn left to walk between the larger buildings above. 'SPALAVERA' is clearly written on a wall. Ignore the path that turns right behind the building, Alpe Colle, and continue straight on.

The way is along a wide, grassy old mule track that was used in WWI. Once clear of the trees it affords good views to the south, including Mottarone above Stresa. You climb the hillside in a series of long zigzags, with the track gradually deteriorating to become a narrow path. Near the summit you enter the **Val Grande National Park**, Italy's largest wilderness area.

Shortly after the park sign you must climb more steeply up into a

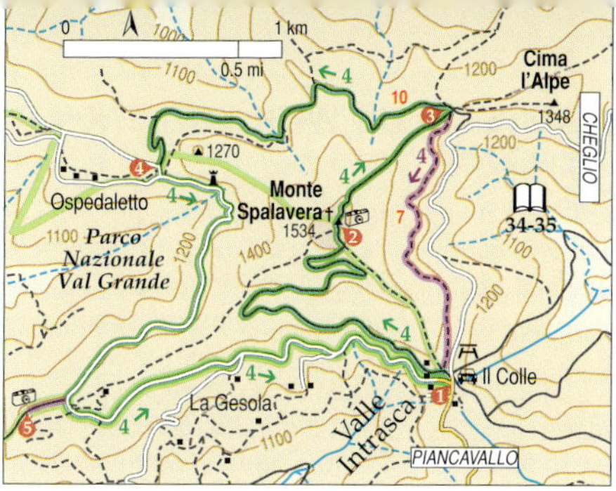

WWI TRENCH SYSTEM. Follow the waymarks through the stone-lined and remarkably well-preserved trenches, to reach the SUMMIT of **Monte Spalavera** (2; **58min**), where there is a cross with an inspirational inscription. There is also an excellent viewpoint indicator that details the northern skyline from Luino in the east to Monte Zeda in the west. However, there is more to see than that! The alpine peak of Monte Rosa is to the southwest and, to the east, Monte Generoso (Walk 14) stands on the Italian/Swiss border between the lakes of Como and Lugano. Clearly visible and nearer at hand are Monte Carza (Walk 1) and Valle Veddasca above Luino (Walks 6 and 7). *(The Short walk returns to Il Colle from here.)*

From the top, pass the viewpoint indicator to follow waymarks off the summit through an area of rhododendrons, which are beautiful when in flower. Notice the wartime bunkers on Cima l'Alpe (a), the hill to your right. You descend through trees, passing more trenches, before reaching a junction of tracks in a flat area at the COL BEFORE **Cima l'Alpe** (3; **1h 18min**). (It is possible to return directly to Il Colle from here by doubling back sharp right along an signposted track through beech woods.

To continue the main walk turn left here on ROUTE 10 and follow a stony track that contours along the mountainside., keeping left at a fork where another path goes straight on. Eventually a gentle incline leads to a grassy clearing where you turn left uphill on the main track, to quickly reach a COL NEAR **Ospedaletto** (4; **1h 50min**). There's a water trough here, but unfortunately the water is undrinkable.

Go straight ahead across the col and down to a wide, well-surfaced track. Turn left and after about eight minutes you will reach a small WWII MEMORIAL to a fallen partisan. In another 18 minutes you leave the tunnel of trees on a wide bend. To your right is a small grassy knoll — a superb VIEWPOINT (5; allow 10 minutes return). Then continue along the track that now gradually descends past a few houses. The surface becomes asphalt just before you return to the CAR PARK at **Il Colle** (1; **2h 47min**).

On the grassy summit of Monte Spalavera

Walk 5: PIZZO PERNICE CIRCUIT WITH EXTENSTION TO I BALMITT (AND IL PIZZO)

Distance: 12.8km/8mi; 4h12min
Grade: ● moderate; on good, waymarked mountain paths, with 780m/2559ft of ascent/descent overall
Note: on some maps I Balmitt is shown as Monte Todano.
Equipment: see page 26. Refreshments available from the Rifugio Pian Cavallone (weekends from May to Oct, daily in Aug)
Transport: 🚘 Follow Car tour 1 to Cambiasca, turn left to Miazzina, then follow signs for Alpe Pala. Keep on this main road until it ends at the car park at Cappella Fina (45° 59.097'N, 8° 31.471'E).
Nearest accommodation: any of the lakeside towns on the western shore of Lake Maggiore
Short walk: Pizzo Pernice circuit. 8.6km/5.3mi; 2h38min. ● Easy-moderate; equipment and access as main walk. Follow the main walk as far as the COL at the 1h53min-point (❺). Turn right here and follow the main walk again from the 3h27min-point to the end.

Breathe in the clear mountain air — you are starting at an altitude of over 1100m/3608ft! This is a great mountain ridge walk, with no difficult climbs, on the edge of the Val Grande National Park, the largest wilderness area in Italy.

Starting from the entrance to the CAR PARK at **Cappella Fina**, take the clearly signposted path towards MOTTA D'AURELIO. Follow this path, ignoring any minor paths to the left or right, as it gently climbs and contours around the mountainside through tall pine trees. Signs of wildlife are clearly evident — foxes, badgers and squirrels — and in autumn it is a popular area with fungi gatherers.

About two minutes after passing a bench you reach a JUNCTION at the edge of the trees (**43min**). Turn right here to go up the zigzags and reach the RIDGE near the tree-

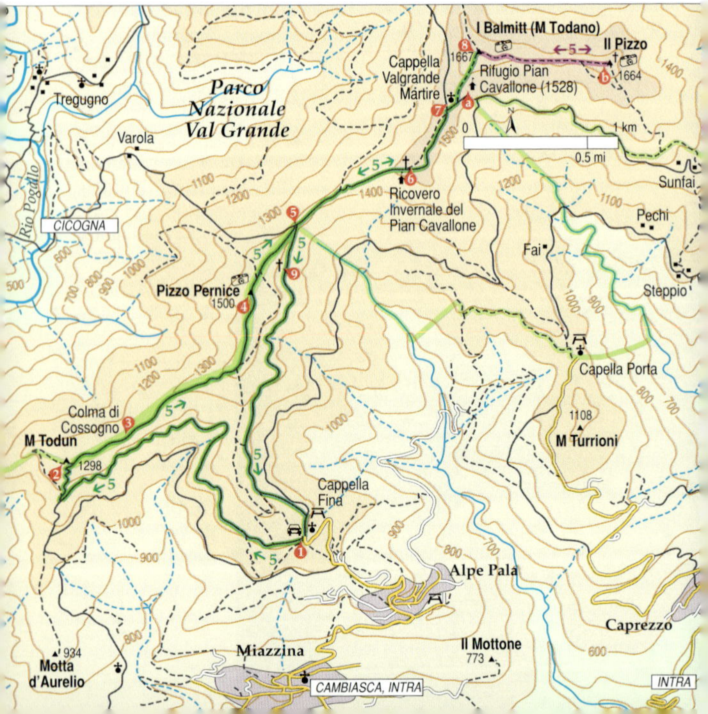

shrouded summit of **Monte Todun** (2; **55min**).

Continue along the ridge in a northwesterly direction, following the waymarked path and the **Val Grande National Park** boundary, to drop down to a col, the **Colma di Cossogno** (3). As you climb up on the far side you can enjoy your first clear views across Val Pogallo into the heart of Val Grande. Below is the remote village of Cicogna. The ascent, on an easy grassy path, is steep at first but ends with a lovely curving ridge walk to the SUMMIT of **Pizzo Pernice** (4; **1h42min**). The views across the Val Pogallo are tremendous, and to the north the rugged Pizzo Marona draws the eye. On the skyline to the right of this lies your objective, the grassy peak of I Balmitt, and laid out before you is the way ahead.

Head down the ridge along the clear path, to a COL. Ignore a path off left to Cicogna and then, shortly after, meet a path doubling back to the right — your eventual return route (5; **1h53min**). *(The Short walk returns from here to Cappella Fina.)*

You now follow an easy section along the ridge and then walk between a stone building, the **Ricovero Invernale del Pian Cavallone** (a winter rescue point) and a tall METAL CROSS (6). Carry on along the ridge, with your objective, I Balmitt, in sight, and descend to the **Cappella Valgrande Martire** (7), a small chapel built in an exposed position on the Pian Cavallone saddle and visible from many mountain walks around the lake. Below and to the right is the **Rifugio Pian Cavallone** (a).

Now climb up the easy slopes to reach the high stone cairn on the SUMMIT of **I Balmitt** (8; **2h47min**). Another wonderful

Signposted path to Cicogna on the col north of Pizzo Pernice

vista awaits you; across the upper reaches of Valle Intrasca lies Monte Spalavera (Walk 4). (From the cairn you could continue by walking out along the ridge over Il Todun to the small WOODEN CROSS on **Il Pizzo** (b), another wonderful viewpoint overlooking the Valle Intrasca. If you do, allow about 40 minutes for the return trip.)

Now retrace your steps back to the COL at the 1h53min-point (5; **3h27min**). Turn left here along the clear, red/white waymarked path, to enter woods and pass a very old SHRINE on the right (9). Emerge from the trees onto a rocky promontory from where you can see the way snaking ahead. Keep on the main path (ignoring a fork to the right after about 30 minutes) and gradually descend, eventually returning to **Cappella Fina** (1; **4h12min**).

Walk 6: FROM BIEGNO TO MACCAGNO

Distance/time: 14km/8.7mi; 4h13min

Grade: ● moderate; mainly on tracks and good — mostly well-waymarked and signposted — paths, with 480m/ 1575ft of ascent and 1200m/ 3937ft of descent

Equipment: see page 26. Walking poles. Refreshments available at Biegno, La Forcola and Maccagno

Transport: From Cannobio to Maccagno and then to Biegno (the 08.01 bus is the most suitable; see 'Transport information' inside the back cover). Allow 12 minutes to walk from the ferry to the bus stop: leave the ferry terminal and walk straight ahead up a narrow road, turning left after 50m along a red cobblestone path between houses and gardens. The path crosses an asphalt road and then twists and turns to reach the main road opposite a church. Turn left and go under the railway bridge. There is an excellent 'Pro Loco' tourist information office on the right just before you cross the Torrente Giona. Continue through the town until you reach Piazza Vittorio Veneto where the bus to Biegno stops. Return on from Maccagno.

Nearest accommodation: Maccagno, Cannobio, Cannero Riviera

Short walk: From La Forcola to Montereccio and back. 5km/3mi; 2h. ● Easy, with an ascent/ descent of 200m/650ft; equipment as above. Access by : from Maccagno drive along the road to Valle Veddasca and follow signs for Musignano. Above this village, bear right to reach **La Forcola** (❺; 46° 4.533'N, 8° 46.664'E) in a further 3.8km/2.3mi. Walk eastwards up the ridge to **Monte Sirti** (❹) and as far as **Montereccio** (❸). Return the same way.

This walk starts from Biegno, far above Maccagno in the lovely Valle Veddasca. You climb up to two isolated hamlets and continue along a beautiful ridge. The long descent back to the lakeside will give you an appreciation of the hardy folk from the hill villages who, until recently, had to carry their provisions up these steep cobbled mule tracks.

From the BUS STOP in **Biegno** (❶) walk along the road in a northerly direction, enjoying views over the rooftops to the village of Monteviasco (Walk 7) across Valle Veddasca. After three minutes turn left up an asphalt road that quickly becomes concrete and is clearly signposted to CANGILI. Leave the road at the first hairpin bend: take a path on the left, signposted 'SENTIERO CANGILI'. This steep path up through the trees quickly leads to an oddly shaped structure (a water station of some sort). Climb the little bank on the far side of this building, indicated by a white arrow, and continue on the path (*not waymarked*, but easily followed). You reach a SHRINE after 15 minutes and, seven minutes later, meet the road again. Turn left to the beautiful hamlet of **Cangili**. The houses here have been renovated, many now being used as holiday homes — it is a most attractive, tranquil place. Follow the road up to the CHURCH (❷; **32min**) where there is a picnic table. The views of the upper reaches of Valle Veddasca are excellent and include the peaks of Monte Gambarogno and Monte Tamaro (which both lie in Switzerland).

Keep on the road, which climbs above the village and then turns

The church in Cangili, above Valle Veddasca

southwest. The walking becomes easier and the route, now on a motorable track, contours and rises gently as it traverses the hillside. Eventually you reach a signposted junction (**1h02min**) from where there are some lovely open views. Turn right, as signposted, and walk up to the hamlet of **Montereccio** (❸; **1h12min**), where again the houses have been restored. Turn left beside a picnic table and water trough, following a sign for MACCAGNO — there is a small yellow, red and white sign, 'SENTIERO', just ahead. Above the hamlet turn left and climb a rough path to the ridge and a SIGNPOSTED JUNCTION.

Turn sharp left here, for PASSO DI FORCOLA and LAGO D'ELIO. This ridge path offers good views to the south and is well waymarked. The red and white paint marks soon lead to a grassy clearing, the COL of **Forcoletta**. Continue straight on and climb **Monte Sirti** (❹; **1h53min**), a fine picnic spot with fabulous views of the Swiss mountains above Locarno, and down to the town of Brissago on the shores of Lake Maggiore.

To continue, drop steeply down to the chapel of **Madonna della Neve** at the wide grassy COL of **La Forcola** (❺; **2h06min**), a popular skiing area. Go to the left of the bar, which is below the chapel, and behind you will find a signposted path to MACCAGNO. The path narrows and enters woodland after passing a building, and follows obvious waymarks (ROUTE 110-3V) down through the trees to reach a track, where you turn left. In another 13 minutes you come to a signposted junction — turn left here for LAGO D'ELIO. Soon you can see this small reservoir just below. Follow the wide and fairly level path until you come to a turning on your right, where waymarks lead down through some trees towards the **Lago d'Elio** (**2h51min**). Do *not* go over the dam, but follow the waymarks across a grassy area and then down to the right, to cross a dry stream bed. Climb the far bank up to a level path and turn left to an asphalt road. Turn left here to meet the road that has descended from Forcola (**3h01min**).

Go down the road for about two minutes and then turn left on a steep cobbled path, signposted to MACCAGNO (still ROUTE 110-3V). You soon meet the road again: turn left and, after 80m, turn right along the cobbled path once more. Keep on this until you reach the narrow streets of **Musignano** (❻;

3h17min). Follow the clear waymarks through this interesting little village to a parking area. Turn right, passing a bus stop, and walk down the road for another two minutes, before bearing right on a cobbled path. After eight minutes you go under an arched SHRINE; four minutes after the next SHRINE you meet a road. Turn right, to the small hamlet of **Sarangio** (**7**; **3h35min**).

The road ends, and the path ahead takes you across a grassy field before entering the trees. Go over an old stone BRIDGE beside a waterfall and, at the next junction, keep straight ahead, soon ignoring a path coming in from the right. In three minutes you reach a road where you turn left uphill, following the waymarks to **Pianca** (**8**; **3h58min**), where the road ends.

Carry on through the PARKING AREA and head down a path that starts beside a small SHRINE. You now descend into the outskirts of Maccagno, enjoying fine views across the rooftops of the town. After passing house No. 5 keep right. Go straight over a road and, at the next junction, turn right to follow the STATIONS OF THE CROSS down to the end of the path in VIA BAROGGIANGELO. At the asphalt road ahead turn right to meet the main road almost opposite the Piazza Vittorio Veneto in **Maccagno** (**9**; **4h13min**).

Walk 7: MONTEVIASCO CIRCUIT FROM CURIGLIA

Distance/time: 11km/6.8m; 3h34min

Grade: 🔴 fairly easy, but with a steep ascent of some 500m/1640ft to Monteviasco and the alms; well waymarked and signposted

Equipment: see page 26. Refreshments are available at the lower cable car station, Monteviasco and Curiglia.

Transport: 🚗 From the north side of Luino follow signs for Dumenza and then Curiglia. Park at the entrance to the village, opposite the bus stop (46° 3.624'N, 8° 48.204'E) — a drive of some 25-30min. Or by ⛴ from Cannobio: take the ferry to Luino. Then go on to Curiglia by 🚌. From the ferry terminal allow five minutes to walk to the bus stop: turn left to walk along the front, past the small harbour. At the first roundabout turn right uphill, signposted for Dumenza. Just beyond the Piazza San Francesco, on the right-hand side of the road, is the bus stop for Curiglia. See 'Transport information' inside the back cover for bus times.

Nearest accommodation: Maccagno, Luino, Cannobio, Cannero Riviera

***Shorter walk*: *Monteviasco by cable car*.** 9km/5.6mi; 2h44min. 🔵 Easy; equipment and access as main walk. Follow the main walk to ❷, then take the cable car to

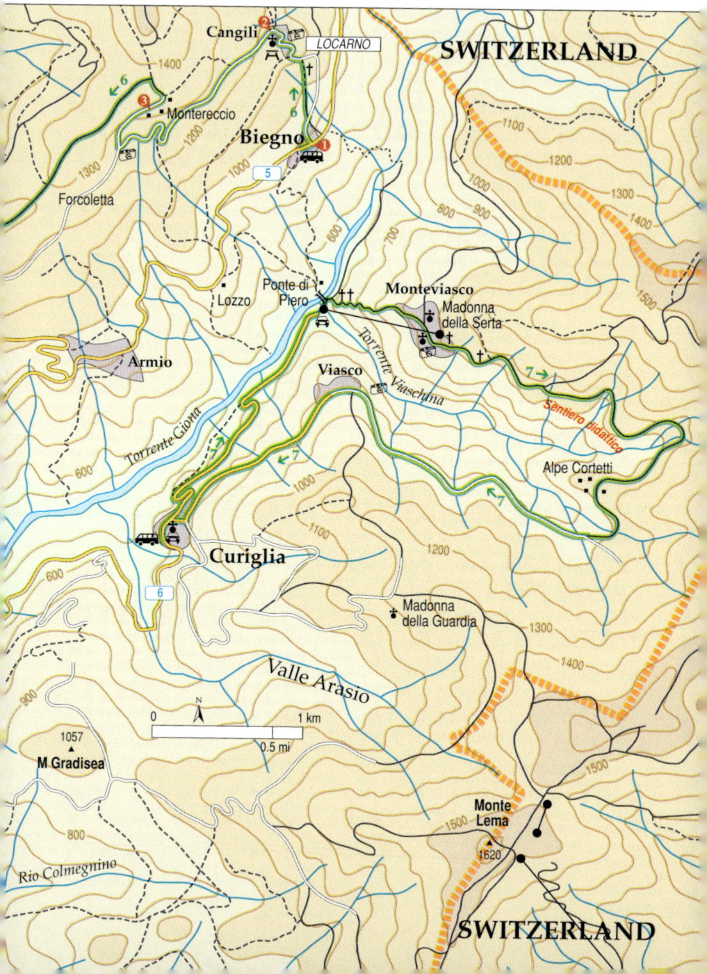

Monteviasco (❸), saving 400m/ 1310ft of ascent. (If you *only* wish to visit and return from Monteviasco, there is ample parking at the lower station.) In summer the cable car runs (Mon-Sat) at 07.00, 09.30, 11.30, 12.15, 15.30, 18.30, 20.30 and (Sun) every hour on the hour. In winter it runs (Mon-Sat) at 07.00, 09.30, 11.30, 12.15, 15.30, 17.30, 19.30, (Sun) at 09.30, 10.00, 11.00, 12.00, 12.30, 14.00, 15.00, 16.00, 17.00, 18.00, 18.30, 20.30.

Make your way up the old mule track to Monteviasco and you enter another world — one with the undisturbed stillness of life without the combustion engine. This is a walk where a calmer, less frenetic lifestyle can be savoured and appreciated.

Start the walk at the BUS STOP/ CAR PARK in **Curiglia** (❶): walk up the road and, at the first junction, bear left downhill (there is a walking sign to MONTEVIASCO). At the next junction take the lower road and walk out of the village. Across Valle Veddasca you can see the houses of Lozzo and Biegno (the start of Walk 6). Continue steadily down to reach a large car park and bar beside the LOWER CABLE CAR STATION FOR MONTEVIASCO (❷; **27min**).

You walk under the cable car wires and cross the **Torrente Viaschina**. Turn right just before the bridge over the Torrente Giona (**Ponte di Piero**), following the signpost for MONTEVIASCO. Start climbing to join the cobbled mule track in a few metres. This old way is in excellent condition, as until fairly recently it was the main access to Monteviasco. The villagers' only other contact with the modern world was the path to Curiglia followed later.

After 34 minutes you come to a second SHRINE and an information board about the wildlife found in this area. Continue up through old terraces, passing a house in nine minutes, and reaching a junction just beyond it. Head right and continue up to a small church with a squat central tower, **Madonna della Serta**. It is in the shape of a Greek cross — with arms of equal length. The interior is painted in bold colours and is surprisingly modern. There are amusing inscriptions on the outside walls and fine views across the valley and the mountains on the far side of Lake Maggiore.

Continue up to the junction by the old CAMPANILE in **Monteviasco** (❸; **1h17min**). Keep straight ahead, down the steps by the side of the CHURCH and, for a great view and possible lunch stop, turn right under an archway to a balcony overlooking the old stone roofs. The church has a very ornate interior and, on an exterior wall, there is an interesting international time check next to a large sundial. Wonderful tranquillity pervades the village. Notice that the houses have a balcony *(lobbie)*, which not only provides breathtaking views, but also affords access to all the rooms.

Return to the bottom of the steps below the campanile and turn right along the narrow street between the houses under the balconies (one house actually bridges the road). At the end of this street there is a bar/restaurant. Look back to see an attractive painting on the wall of a house — you will see others further on. Nearby is a public toilet. Now follow the sign for VIASCO and CURIGLIA, indicating your onward route — along another narrow street at the left of the bar. When you come to a SHRINE at a junction, follow the paint waymarks to the left uphill and leave the village. Ford a small stream and head into the trees, soon passing a few houses and farm buildings, and climb up to a SHRINE atop a rocky viewpoint (**1h33min**).

Continue on to quickly reach a JUNCTION (4) where you bear right. (The path to the left winds up to the Swiss border, which is on the skyline ahead.) You will see several information boards along the next part of the walk around the steep valley of the **Torrente Viaschina**, passing two ruined alms. Even with a limited knowledge of Italian you should find them interesting, as the drawings aid understanding.

The path leads to a BRIDGE across a cascading stream and in another 14 minutes you descend a short distance to ford a fast-flowing stream. Go on to round the head of the valley, passing a small old building that was once used for cheese-making, and continue up to the deserted and ruined buildings of a third alm, **Alpe Cortetti** (5; **2h19min**).

From here descend steeply for 10 minutes, to cross another stream by a ford (or a rickety old bridge). After one more stream crossing you join a wide track and carry on through well-managed beech woods. Follow this track in an easy descent. Eventually, just before you leave the woods, there is a fine view through the trees across the deep valley to Monteviasco: from here it looks like a Tibetan village perched on the mountainside. Then you reach the small, scattered village of **Viasco** (6; **3h09min**).

You leave Viasco on an asphalt road that you follow, sometimes steeply, all the way to **Curiglia** (1; **3h34min**).

View from Monteviasco over Valle Veddasca

Walk 8: FROM MOTTARONE STATION TO CARCIANO DI STRESA

See also photograph page 16
Distance/time: 11.2km/7mi; 2h58min
Grade: ● easy, but long, descent of 1300m/4265ft. Well signposted and waymarked (Route L1)
Equipment: see page 26. Walking sticks. Refreshments are available on Mottarone and at Levo.
Transport: 🚗 or on foot to the *funivia* (cable car station) in the Piazzale Lido at Carciano di Stresa (45° 53.444'N, 8° 31.499'E). To get there from the Stresa ferry terminal walk northwest along the front. Then 🚡 to Mottarone station (every 20 minutes from 09.30-12.30 and 13.30-17.30).
Nearest accommodation: Stresa
Short walks: The main walk can be split conveniently into two easy but differing sections. We especially recommend Short walk 2, as this is the more interesting and has better views.

1 From Mottarone Station to Alpino Station. 6.2km/3.8mi; 1h38min. ● Easy; equipment and access as above. Follow the main walk to the 1h38min-point at **Alpino Station** (4). Return by cable car to **Carciano di Stresa** (9).

2 Alpino Station to Carciano di Stresa. 5km/3mi; 1h20min. ● Grade and equipment as above. Access: take the 🚡 to the **Alpino Station** (4) and follow the main walk from the 1h38min-point down to **Carciano** (9).

Alternative walk: Far side of Mottarone. 4.5km/2.8mi; 1h30min. ● Grade, equipment, access as for the main walk. Follow the main walk to the SUMMIT OF **Mottarone** (2). Go to the left of the tallest telecommunications mast and walk down towards the bars and car park. Bear left by the small gift shop and cross the road, heading towards another trio of masts. A path leads along the ridge that stretches out ahead, signposted to PALESTRA DI ROCCIA. Follow this until you come to a ROCKY AREA (a) that overlooks Lake Orta — a haven for rock climbers. There are magnificent views from here. Return the same way to the three masts and then either walk back over the summit or turn left along the road to the top station (1).

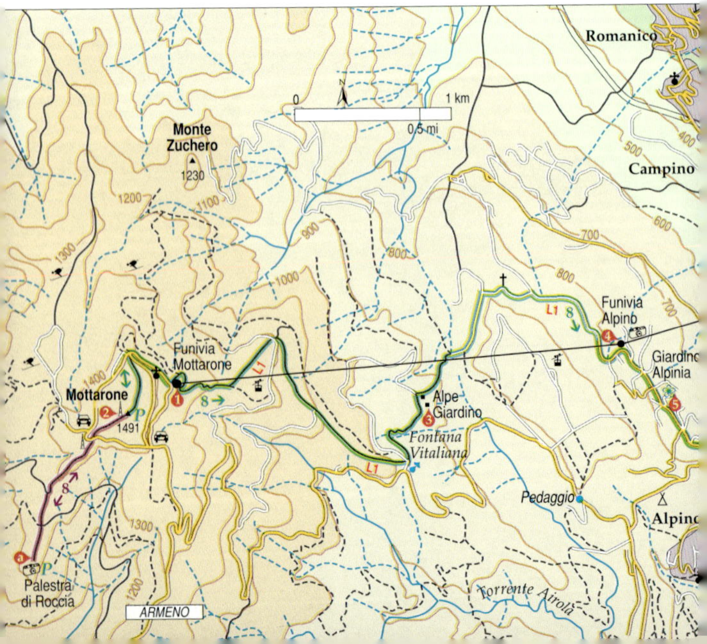

Mottarone, the mountain that rises behind Stresa, is one of the most beautiful and extensive viewpoints around Lake Maggiore, and it is certainly the most accessible. The grassy hillsides around the summit are an invitation for easy rambles, and the long descent is not difficult — offering much of interest, especially on the lower section.

Start the walk at the MOTTARONE CABLE CAR STATION *(funivia)* (**1**): turn right by the Bar Alpe Eden and follow the asphalt road up to a junction. Go straight across and follow the well-used path to the summit of **Mottarone** (**2**; **17min**). Ignoring the intrusive masts and skiing paraphernalia, enjoy the open spaces with far-reaching views that encompass a huge arc of the Alps, dominated by Monte Rosa in the west. Far below, Lake Maggiore is spread out before you and, on a clear day, you may even see Milan.

Return to the CABLE CAR STATION (**1**; **29min**). From here the walk to Stresa is well waymarked with YELLOW **'L1'** SIGNS and begins to the left of the station, where you take a narrow path dropping around the front of the building, underneath the cables. This route is popular with mountain bikers, so listen out for them as they hurtle down towards you. In 11 minutes a sign points you up a little bank, and on the far side the path continues downhill along a ridge, affording views over the wooded flanks of Mottarone. You pass under the cable car wires again and come to a crossroads, where you keep straight on to go under the wires once more. Follow the stony path at a steady

Alpino station and cable car (left) and church at Levo (below)

angle until you reach a junction by an old pink building and parking area, near the **Fontana Vitaliana** (**1h09min**).

Turn left (well signposted) and in nine minutes, after crossing a small stream, you reach the ruined buildings of **Alpe Giardino** (3). Keep right here and continue on the clear path. In thinning trees a track joins from the left just before you enter a wide, open area that you cross, going beneath the cable car wires yet again. On the far side bear left, joining a track coming from the right. In about seven minutes you meet another junction where you bear right — a little further on look out for a dilapidated, but still cared for, SHRINE. At a road keep straight on under the *funivia* to approach a farm in open pasture. The now-asphalted road leads down to the ALPINO CABLE CAR STATION (4; **1h38min**), from where there are good views across the lake, and this grassy area is a pleasant spot for a break. *(Short walk 1 ends here, and Short walk 2 begins here.)*

Continue along the road, coming to a high leylandi hedge that shelters the **Giardino Alpinia** (5; the Alpine Botanical Garden). Six minutes later you reach the entrance and car park. A visit is a must if you would like to admire the extensive range of alpine plants and shrubs that grow in these beautiful gardens.

In a further eight minutes, after passing some impressive homes, leave the asphalt road by a house called ALPE PINA (6). Turn left here, dropping steeply for a short way and enjoying the fine views. When you reach a concrete track, turn left, initially through a tunnel of trees, and then follow a wide path below the garden of a large house, to meet a narrow asphalt road. Along here there are excellent views over the rooftops of Levo and all the way down to Stresa. Coming to a junction, turn right downhill, passing a bar. At the main village road in **Levo** (7; **2h11min**), and almost opposite, is a short flight of steps by the Bar Sport. Go down these to the attractive old church shown on page 53, painted a creamy yellow with large murals on its walls. Around the building, and donated by village families, are several shrines depicting biblical scenes.

Keep to the left of the church, on the asphalt road, to reach a junction with the main road on a hairpin bend. Go right for a short distance and then, just after the ALBERGO CASA DI SOGGIORNO, turn right (a short cut). When you meet the main road again, cross over and, at a junction, go straight ahead beneath the *funivia*. After the last house continue on a path, to reach another small CHURCH hidden in the trees. Turn sharply right here down the cobbled road into **Someraro** (8; **2h28min**).

Go straight across the main road,

then turn right by house No. 24. Keep left at a fork and wind downhill along the narrow street to the church, which has an unusual belfry. From here you can look over the rooftops to the beautiful Isola Madre with Pallanza beyond.

You now descend VIA PER STRESA and, after roughly 15 minutes, you meet the main road again. Turn left and walk around the first bend to find signs pointing to your path, which immediately joins an asphalt road. This road drops steeply down between the elegant houses of **Carciano di Stresa**.

Take the first right, along VIA SAN BIAGIO, and then the first left, to walk in front of a large CHURCH on your right. Cross the RAILWAY BRIDGE and carry on to the main road that runs between Baveno and Stresa. Go straight across and walk down to **Lake Maggiore** and the PIAZZALE LIDO (9; **2h58min**).

View to Isola Bella from the Piazzale Lido at Carciano di Stresa

The Borromean influence

The name Borromeo *has long been associated with Lake Maggiore. From the 15th century onwards this famous banking family have poured money into the area. Carlo Borromeo III seized two of the islands on the lake, displacing the resident fishing families, built a palace full of extravagant features and started to create the amazing and exotic gardens of Isola Bella. This island he named after his wife, Isabella. On Isola Madre family members built a villa surrounded by more beautiful gardens and here you will find the Borromean tombs. Isola Pescatori remains the 'Island of the Fishermen', after whom it is named.*

Later generations became concerned with culture and the preservation of their forebears' historic and artistic heritage. They also introduced schools that influenced the Italian education system until the 1960s.

Walk 9: FROM BELGIRATE TO STRESA

Distance/time: 8.7km/5.4mi; 2h29min
Grade: ● easy, but with an ascent of 325m/1066ft
Equipment: see page 26. Trainers will suffice. Refreshments are available at Magognino.
Transport: ferry, train or bus from Stresa to Belgirate and back
Nearest accommodation: Stresa

This beautiful walk is full of interest. It follows the Stresa tourist board's 'Chestnut Trail' (Route L2, with 12 information boards), but in the *opposite direction,* to take advantage of better facilities and more frequent transport at the end.

Start from the FERRY TERMINAL in **Belgirate** (1): walk a short way south along the waterfront. Cross the main road and climb the 76 steps that start next to the front of the CHURCH. At the top turn left by a children's play area. Wind along VIA ELENA CONELLI, past an old WASHHOUSE with a little SHRINE set in an alcove. At the end of the street cross the road to the train station, go under the RAILWAY BRIDGE, and then turn right. You will see a bell tower ahead and a right turn will take you up to the church of **Santa Maria** (Chiesa Vecchia), which has a red-tiled roof and a stone-built Romanesque campanile (**10min**). Adjacent is a beautifully kept CEMETERY, from where there are good views over the town and across to the eastern shores of Lake Maggiore.

Shrine on the outskirts of Stresa

A red/white sign to the left of the church, 'L2 BELGIRATE — STRESA', points you along a steep path that climbs up beside the graveyard to the driveways of two houses. Take the signposted path that goes up between No 33 (left) and 12 (right), soon coming to a rather unusual SHRINE dedicated to San Sebastiano. Continue up to an asphalt road, where you turn right and then, almost immediately, left on a path with a red/white 'L2' sign. Climb past a track going off to the left, and you will meet a road again.

Go straight across, at the right of a house (sign: CALOGNA), and keep up the path through chestnut woods at the side of a small stream, which you cross on an old BRIDGE (2). The path rises alongside the garden of a large house, to come to an old SHRINE. Bear right here, and shortly after meet an asphalt road. Follow this to a junction, then keep right on a wider road that passes the village old WASHING PLACE and winds through the streets of **Calogna**. At the T-junction where the road sign points back to 'LESA 5', turn right, to arrive at the CHURCH (3; **46min**). Your climbing is now all but done — this is perhaps a good time to take a break! There are commemorative stones on the steps up to the church, with a tree planted by each one — the village's tribute to its war dead, a moving sight.

Returning from the church, turn sharp right (signed, red/white waymarks). In about 10 minutes waymarks take you off the main route to the chapel of **San Paolo** (4) then, some 20 minutes later, you pass another chapel, **San Grato** (5), with prehistoric petroglyphs. Tar comes underfoot, and you reach a road: follow it to the left and pass the front of the church of **San Albino** in **Magognino** (3; **1h34min**). Built in

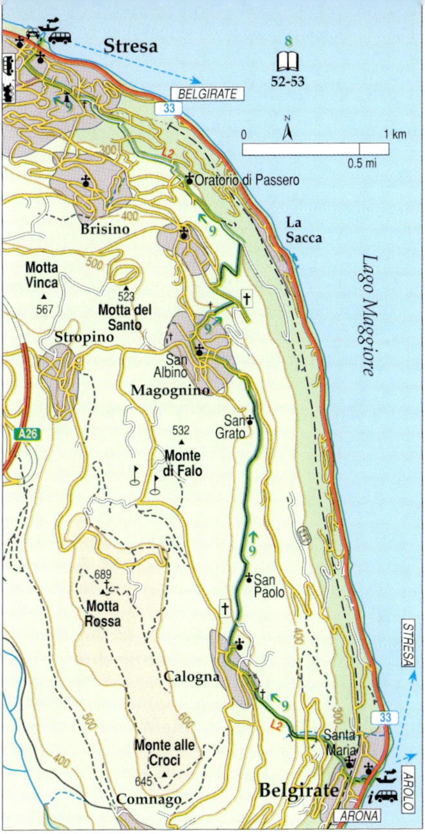

1773, the church has two brightly coloured mosaics displayed on its facade.

With your back to the church, turn right along the street with the STOP SIGN. Turn right at the end of this street, keeping to the left of the POST OFFICE, and proceed downhill through this quiet village. After a right-hand bend, take the narrow asphalt road that descends steeply to the right (just before a 'STRESA 5' road sign). The road becomes a wide track after a few houses and, crossing a stream, turns into a cobbled path, which you follow down to **Brisino**'s CEMETERY (7). Turn left along the level asphalt road, continue on past houses and look for a RED/WHITE SIGN that directs you around a right-hand bend at a junction. Shortly after, around a left-hand bend, turn right down another RED/WHITE MARKED PATH. At the bottom of its descent, turn left at a multiple JUNCTION. You pass a ruin and then keep straight ahead beside a large house, after which asphalt comes under foot. Follow this road to a fork, then bear right, down to the small **Oratorio di Passero** (8; **2h 08min**).

Just beyond the church turn right on a signposted wide grassy track, with a beautiful view to Isola Madre. Cross the asphalt road at the bottom to carry on along another track. Beyond house No. 5 contin ue on an old cobbled path that meets a cobbled driveway by the entrance to a house. Follow this, descending to a junction where there is a SHRINE behind you. Go down the wide asphalt road here, passing a beautiful MEMORIAL on the left. At the bottom of the incline, *to walk to the ferry:** bear right through a parking area and turn left down the road with the NO ENTRY SIGN. At its end, go straight ahead into the pedestrian area to arrive at the PIAZZA CADORNA. Keep right here, straight along to the waterfront opposite the FERRY TERMINAL/BUS STOP in **Stresa** (9; **2h29min**).

*To reach the train station, go half left on the road signed to MILANO. Keep straight on to where the raised railway line is ahead, then curve right towards STAZIONE. There is also a BUS STOP at the STATION (**2h30min**).

Walk 10: CIRCUIT FROM AGRANO VIA ALPE SELVIANA

Distance/time: 8.4km/5.2mi; 2h32min
Note: The gate at Alpe Selviana is only open from 13.00-19.30 in the season, after 31/8 on weekends only. To get to the Torrente Pescone out of season, it is possible to walk further up the road and make your way through a farm down to the path to the gorge.
Grade: ● easy; mainly on quiet country tracks and woodland paths, with 450m/1476ft of ascent/descent
Equipment: see page 26. Refreshments are available at Alpe Selviana and Pratolungo.
Transport: 🚗 Follow Car tour 2 or, for a more direct route, leave Car tour 2 at Gignese to drive through the village and on to Armeno. From here follow signs for Agrano and pick up Car tour 2 again. Park at Agrano's car park, just past the church, by the sports ground at the start of Via Giulio Isotta (45° 50.749'N, 8° 24.845'E)
Nearest accommodation: Stresa or Orta San Giulio
Short walk: Waterfalls circuit. 3.8km/2.3mi; 1h08min. ● Easy, with only 150m/490ft ascent/descent overall. Access and equipment as main walk. Follow the main walk to Pescone and, at the 56min-point, keep straight along the road to return to Agrano.

An easy walk that is a real gem! A beautiful river cascades into sparkling pools — perfect for a cooling dip, so take your swimsuit. Later, a steep climb brings you to a marvellous viewpoint above Lake Orta — what more could a relatively short walk provide?

The walk begins near the centre of **Agrano**: leave the CAR PARK (1) and turn right along VIA GIULIO ISOTTA, with the school on your right. Keep right by the end of the road and come to the Piazza Maggio. Opposite, at the left of the large arcaded building, you will see a sign for ALPE SELVIANA, pointing you up an alley of the same name. Follow this alley out of the village, gently rising. At a junction with a sign for MOTTARONE, keep right and, just a few metres on, keep left for SELVIANA. Continue on the asphalt road, ignoring a first turn-off on the right. Then pass a second turn-off to the right (2; you will descend this path later).

Take time to look at the appealing modern MEMORIAL SHRINE just before the entrance to **Alpe Selviana** (**23min**), then go through the gateway and walk down to the front of the buildings. The museum and bio restaurant are open from 13.00-19.30 daily during the season, with various products from their organic farm for sale. Beyond the buildings, follow a grassy track and then a path into a field, where there will probably be various livestock around, including pigs, turkeys

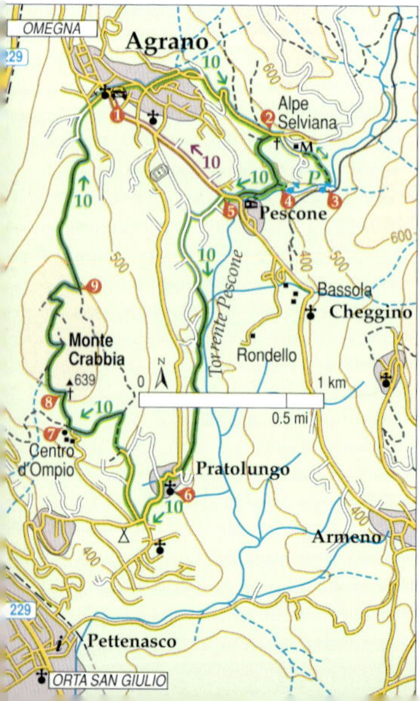

and ducks. The path leads into some trees and down to the side of a gorge. Descend to the **Torrente Pescone** and the pool of your choice. The water cascades gracefully over smooth rocks into crystal-clear pools, before a final slide takes it out of sight into the deep gorge below. It's an idyllic spot for sunbathing and a swim (3; **31min**; Picnic 5).

Return through Alpe Selviana to the road and, retracing your steps for about two minutes, take the path on the left, which *may* be signposted to PESCONE *(mountain bikers use this path — so be careful)*. Continue downhill to a junction. Turn sharp left (there may be another PESCONE signpost here), soon crossing a small stream and going under a PIPELINE. Just after a

Waterfall at the Torrente Pescone near Alpe Selviana (Picnic 5)

Detail from the memorial shrine near Alpe Selviana

sign warning bikers to slow down, there was a mattress attached to a fence when we were last here — for bikers who did not slow down! From here you can see a WATERFALL through the trees. A little further along, a path doubles back and leads to the foot of this fall. The river spills gently over the high cliff into a large pool — another beautiful spot (4; **51min**).

Return to the main path and carry on until it ends beside a house near the main valley road and bridge in **Pescone** (**55min**). On the other side of the river there is a small HYDROELECTRIC STATION. Turn right up the road and, in one minute, just beyond a house, turn left along a two-wheel gravel track — waymarked by an arrow on a telegraph pole (5; **56min**). *(But for the Short walk, keep straight on here.)*

You quickly enter agricultural land. Ignore a track forking left beside a large building, and carry on by a 'fence' of upright stone slabs, to reach a junction. Turn sharp left here. After passing a large house behind a HIGH METAL FENCE, you meet another junction, where fork left (it should be signposted to PRATOLUNGO). Follow this rough track above the still-tumbling river and then through a field, ablaze with colourful flowers during spring and summer. Ford a stream and come to another, larger, grassy area, where the track starts to climb gently up into the woods.

After you cross a bridge you reach **Pratolungo** (6; **1h23min**) and meet an asphalt road, the VIA PRINCIPALE. Turn left and walk up through the village, passing the small CHURCH and an old WASHHOUSE. Keep left at the junction just past the washhouse; then, after 250m, at the next junction, turn right by an hotel and immediately right again, up VIA REGIONE BARRO (there is a bar here, on the opposite side of this road). Keep steeply uphill on this red/white-waymarked asphalt road (keeping right at a fork) and, when it ends, continue ahead on a track. After 100m this turns sharp left uphill and after another 100m runs between a metal gate and a concrete waterhouse. Continue through woodland until, in sight of an 'igloo' in the New Age seminar centre CENTRO D'OMPIO (7), you turn righton a red/white waymarked path by a 'CROCE' (Cross) sign. Climbing steeply uphill to **Monte Crabbia** (shown on some Italian maps as Monte Barro), you reach the large wooden CROSS (8; **1h58min**) on a rocky promontory overlooking the town of Pettenasco and Lake Orta. Across the lake is Pella (Walk 11; Picnic 6), and to your left lies the hillside town of Armeno.

From this viewpoint follow the clear path some 250m to a T-junction, where you turn right. Shortly after, go left at a fork (both turns are signed). After another 450m there is another T-junction, where you again go right. Five minutes later, at a fork, turn sharp left at the sign for AGRANO (9). You now drop steadily, to eventually pass a large CEMETERY and reach the main road in **Agrano**. Turn right to walk by the CHURCH and return to your car (1; **2h32min**).

Walk 11: CIRCUIT ABOVE LAKE ORTA

Distance/time: 10km/6.3mi; 2h37min
Grade: easy, but with a moderate climb of about 280m/920ft. No waymarking, but easily followed
Equipment: see page 26. No refreshments en route
Transport: Follow Car tour 2 to Pella and park off the main road, beyond the church and near the bridge over the Torrente Pellino (45° 48.100'N, 8° 23.077'E). Or from Orta San Giulio (limited service; be sure to check the current timetable).
Nearest accommodation: Orta San Giulio
***Short walk*: Ronco Inferiore.** 5.8km/3.6mi; 1h20min. Easy, gentle ups and downs. Equipment and access as above. Follow the main walk to Ronco Inferiore. Return the same way, or take the ferry back to Pella via Orta San Giulio.

Savour the serenity of Lake Orta, a lovely and less developed lake than its larger neighbour, Lake Maggiore. This walk, along the western shore and up to the appealing traditional villages on the hillsides above, can easily be combined with a visit to the captivating town of Orta San Giulio and the enchanting island of same name (photograph pages 14-15).

Begin the walk in **Pella** (1): walk out of the village along the road, in a northerly direction. This very quiet road has some fine views across Lake Orta and you will follow it to Ronco Inferiore, your first objective. In 12 minutes you reach a lakeside picnic area which has a lovely outlook to Isola di San Giulio (Picnic 6a). Continue on, shaded by chestnut trees, to eventually reach the village of **Ronco Inferiore**. From the far end of the car park, walk down a narrow street to the WATERFRONT (2; **40min**), where you can relax on one of the benches and appreciate the tranquillity of this lake, which has Mottarone as a backdrop. Explore the tight-knit streets, too narrow for cars, and enjoy this beautiful secluded village to the full. *(The Short walk returns from here.)*

To continue, return to the CAR PARK and find a cobbled path that climbs up alongside the CEMETERY, to a junction overlooked by a SHRINE. Keep right beside a small stream, and then cross it. This old cobbled path up the steep hillside is easy to follow, but *not* way-marked. Pass another SHRINE and keep ahead to the houses of **Ronco Superiore** (3; **1h**), where the angle of ascent eases. Avoid a path off to the right and walk around to the front of a small 17th-century CHAPEL.

Now on a concrete path, you rise past a house on the left. Turn left behind this building and keep climbing, the path becoming a track and then an asphalt road (just before a sharp right-hand bend). Stay on this road to reach a

Ronco Inferiore (Picnic 6b)

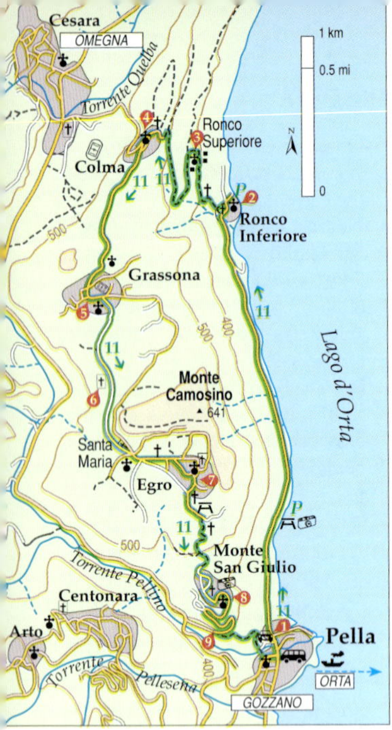

SHRINE at a junction, where you bear left and head down to the front of the CHURCH in **Colma** (4; **1h17min**).

Turn left here up VIA GRASSONA, quickly passing a garden with little statues of Snow White and the Seven Dwarfs — a theme also depicted on the wall of the house! Carry on up the now-wider road, at an easy gradient, through thicker woodland. You enter **Grassona** and drop down into the centre of this village on a wide bend (5; **1h32min**).

Keep left along the main road and then turn right to the CHURCH. Walk along VIA VECCHIA PER EGRO (the old 'road' between Grassona and Egro), after eight minutes passing a small CEMETERY. This attractive route then takes you through pleasant beech woods. In a further 10 minutes the track leads to the church of **Santa Maria** and another small CEMETERY, then joins the asphalt road. Here, turn right on VIA PIANO D'EGRO. This road curves around to the left through open fields and orchards, and passes an attractive SHRINE. Turn right down VIA R. RAMPONI, to enter the quiet, unspoilt village of **Egro** and, at the bottom of the street, turn left up to the CHURCH (7; **1h57min**).

In Piazza San Camillo, at the front of the church, turn right and then immediately left down VIA BELVEDERE, continuing downhill beside a walled orchard and between two attractive old buildings (No. 8 on the right). Shortly after, at a SHRINE by building No. 17, keep left, still on Via Belvedere. You now walk through a small area of farmed land, where you may see some belled cows, to the end of the road. At the T-junction at the end of Via Belvedere, go left. This road passes a picnic area, the asphalt runs out and a you head down an old cobbled path through woods. The lake can be seen below through the trees and you soon pass another SHRINE.

When the path meets a narrow asphalt road, follow it to the right, to a junction with an old SHRINE at the houses of **Monte San Giulio** (8). Bear left here to continue down another road, enjoying the lovely views over Lake Orta and up to Madonna del Sasso, perched on the cliffs above. After 15 minutes, and just before meeting a road junction, watch for your ongoing route: it's a TWO-WHEELED TRACK (9) cutting back to the left. The track descends gently, but then changes to a cobbled path and drops more steeply. Crossing an ancient humpbacked footbridge over the **Torrente Pellino**, you enter **Pella**, and soon you reach the old church with its much newer campanile. Walk downhill from here to the main road, where you turn left to cross the river once more, and return to your starting point (1; **2h37min**).

Walk 12: THREE WALKS BY THE PARCO VAL SANAGRA

See map pages 64-65
Distance, Grade, Transport: see Walks a-c below
Equipment: see page 26
Nearest accommodation: Menaggio

Walk a: Circuit above Lago di Piano. 15.5km/9.6mi; 4h26min
Grade: ● easy; mainly on tracks and country roads, but long, and with about 500m/1640ft of ascent/descent. Good signposting. Refreshments are available at Loveno, Codogna and Naggio.
Transport: 🚗 (Car tour 3) or 🚌 to Menaggio; park near Piazza Garibaldi (46° 1.173'N, 9° 14.323'E) where the bus stops and the walk begins; see 'Transport information' inside the back cover.
Alternative start: 🚗 or 🚌 to Codogna and start there (see Walk b for transport information).

Walk b: From Codogna to Sass Corbee and return. 4.4km/2.7mi; 1h03min. **Grade:** ● easy; mainly on tracks and country roads; short section on riverside path. ! You must be sure-footed if you venture onto the staircase at Sass Corbee. Refreshments are available at Chiodera. Transport: 🚗 Follow Car tour 3 from Menaggio towards Lugano. Turn right after Croce for Grandola Ed Uniti, then fork left through Cardano (a district), to reach Codogna. Park by the war memorial in Piazza Camozzi (46° 1.843'N, 9° 12.536'E), where there is also a bus stop. 🚌 Limited bus service to Codogna (and Naggio); see 'Transport information' inside the back cover.

Walk c: Val Sanagra circuit to Madri. 13.3km/8.2mi; 3h57min. ● ! Moderate, with 550m/1800ft of ascent; well waymarked. You must be sure-footed and have a head for heights. Refreshments are available at Loveno, Codogna, Chiodera and Naggio. Transport as Walk a.

For this walk we offer you several alternative outings. It is easy to avoid the stiff climb out of Menaggio followed in Walks a and c by driving to Codogna, as in Walk b — and in fact all three walks could start in Codogna. The Torrente Sanagra has much of historic interest: old bridges, mills and factories speak of a bygone age; be sure to visit the museum in the Villa Camozzi off the piazza in Codogna to learn more about this whole area. Walk a, which deviates to the west from the river, runs past Il Rogolone, an enormous ancient oak tree with more stories to tell: it was once a meeting place where local issues were debated. Soon you enjoy views over Val Menaggio — and an unsurpassed vista across lakes Piano and Lugano. Walks b and c keep to the Torrento Sanagra and follow the river past old mills to Sass Corbee, a massive rock. Walk b turns back here, while Walk c — the toughest of the three walks, goes upstream to discover beautiful Alpe Madri.

Walk a begins in Piazza Garibaldi in **Menaggio** (1): walk up VIA CALVI, with its book/souvenir shops and cafés, towards the large pink and white church of **San Stefano**. Cross the main road, to find VIA ENRICO CARDONTI DA BLEVIO on the left-hand side of the church. Walk up this short street and then turn right on VIA LEONE LEONI. At the next junction take the left fork up VIA CASTELLINO DA CASTELLO. Follow this cobbled street to the right of a grotto and

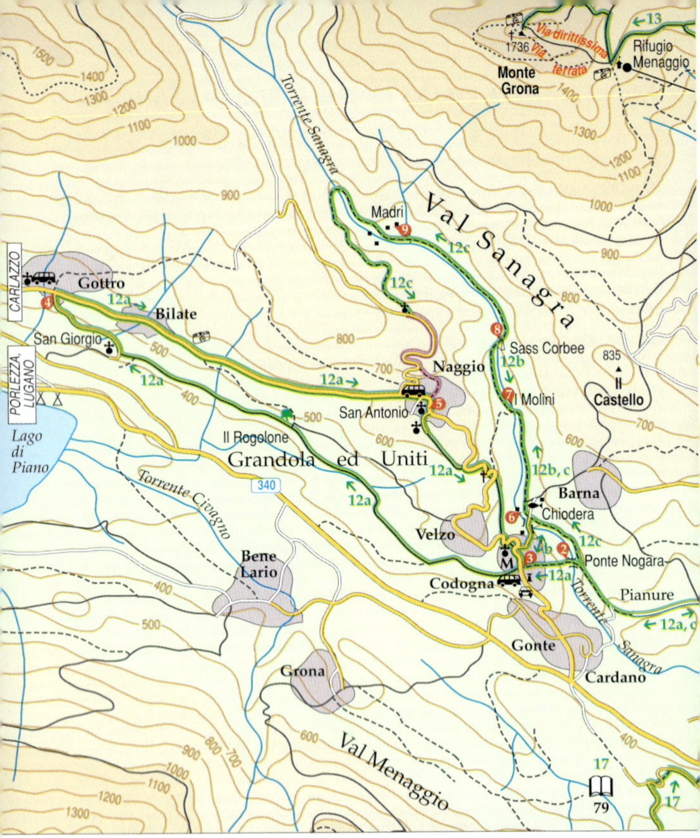

Via dirittissima
Via ferrata
1736
Monte Grona
Rifugio Menaggio
13
Torrente Sanagra
Val Sanagra
Madri
12c
Gottro
12a
Bilate
CARLAZZO
San Giorgio
PORLEZZA, LUGANO
Naggio
San Antonio
Sass Corbee
835
Il Castello
12b
I Molini
Lago di Piano
Il Rogolone
Grandola ed Uniti
340
Torrente Civagno
12b, c
Barna
Chiodera
Velzo
Codogna
Ponte Nogara
Pianure
12a, c
Bene Lario
Gonte
Cardano
Grona
Val Menaggio
17
79

after 150m under an ARCHWAY (on the left are the ruins of the castle, but they are not readily visible from the path), to reach the church of **San Carlo**, built in 1614 (**10min**). Note the beautifully carved wooden doors and the simplicity of the interior.

Continue past the church, to an asphalt road. Cross over and turn right, downhill. Cross the bridge that spans the deep gorge of the **Torrente Sanagra** (often spelled 'Senagra'). Carry on along this busy road to the HOTEL LOVENO and walk up VIA SAURO, a path on the far side of the building, to cut out a bend. Further up the road, at a junction, turn left for PIANURE. This road soon becomes cobbled and winds its way through **Loveno**. Turn left at the top of the street on an asphalt road towards PIANURE (by the Hotel Royal). You have now left the busy town behind, and the quiet countryside beckons. Keep on to the baroque yellow church of **San Lorenzo**. Bear left here and walk steeply uphill, past a SPORTS CENTRE, to eventually reach the flat pasture of **Pianure** at the end of the asphalt road (**39min**).

Go straight on beyond the barrier along the level gravel road. Walk through a small wood and then up beside fields and vines to reach the crest of a spur. At the junction keep straight on, dropping down to a small bridge (PONTE NOGARA) over the **Torrente Sanagra** (❷; **55min**). *(Walk c keeps right here along the river.)* Cross this bridge and follow the cobbled path steeply uphill and then through open pasture. Entering **Codogna**, you reach the Piazza Camozzi (❸; **1h07min**). *(Walk b begins here, and this is an Alternative starting point for Walks a or c.)* Opposite

View to lakes Piano and Lugano on the ascent to Naggio

the WAR MEMORIAL, and across the road, beside the BUS STOP, take the right-hand, minor road called VIA ALLA SANTA, clearly signposted to ROGOLONE. (But before doing so, hopefully you will have time to stop at Villa Camozzi just above it, to learn more about this area.)
You soon pass an old WASHHOUSE where there are good views across the valley. The tarmac peters out into a path, rough in places but well signposted; it continues through pasture and old terraces. After 10 minutes, at a fork beside an old building, bear right, to continue through shady woodland. In another 20 minutes you ford a small stream beside a rickety old gate. A short but latterly steep climb brings you to a grassy clearing and the beautifully shaped proud old oak, **Il Rogolone** (**1h44min**). This lovely tree, more than 25m high, and with a circumference of 8m, offers welcome shade on a hot sunny day.
From Il Rogolone follow the path at the lower side of the clearing (signposted to GOTTRO), to go through a gate. In about 10 minutes, when you reach some signposts, continue straight on for CHIESA DI S GIORGIO. After another nine minutes ignore a stepped (and unsigned) path off left. Two minutes later, you come to a paved road just before the church of **San Giorgio**. Turn left to visit this old medieval building with its beautifully kept graveyard and frescoed interior (if the door is locked, peek in through a window).
Follow the road from the church across the bridge and then uphill to **Gottro** (❹; **2h18min**). Turn right on the asphalt road, passing some large attractive houses as you go through **Bilate**, and then rise steadily towards Naggio. Along the way you come to a marvellous viewpoint overlooking lakes Piano and Lugano. Rising more steeply now, look to your left as you enter **Naggio**, to see the craggy summit of Monte Grona (Walk 13) towering above. Turn right at the first junction, pass the WASHHOUSE, and walk down to the church, **San Antonio** (❺; **3h06min**). If you have time, do explore the narrow streets of this charming village.
From the front of the church, walk down the road. Shortly, keep right at a fork, along VIA DOSSELLO (ignore the sign to Menaggio). Go to the left of another church along STRADA VECCHIA PER CODOGNA. This road quickly becomes a path. You rejoin the asphalt road after about nine minutes: turn right and, between the third and fourth hairpin bends, turn left off the road on an old mule track (a short cut). Go straight across the road by a SHRINE, and follow the grassy path to cross the road again, following VIA VECCHIA MULETTIERA through fields, to the CHURCH in **Codogna**. Cross the road once more and walk down the cobbled path, past the church, to meet the road opposite a SPORTS FIELD. Turn right, walk down to Piazza Camozzi (❸; **3h31min**), and then retrace your steps to **Menaggio** (❶; **4h26min**).

Start Walk b at the WAR MEMORIAL in **Cadogna** (❸): walk up the main village road and take the first right turn (VIA MOLINI). Keep on the asphalt road, past a bar, and then walk down the steep-sided valley. You cross the **Torrente Sanagra** at **Chiodera** (❻). *(Walk c joins here.)* Go to the right of the buildings, once a nail factory but now a restaurant, and walk up beside the TROUT FARM. The steep cliffs of Monte Grona (Walk 13) loom ahead. Beyond an art gallery, continue on the shady path past a weir. At **I Molini** ('The Mills'; ❼)

Walk c: crossing the Torrente Sanagra above Madri and (right) wall painting on a ruin in the hamlet

you cross an old ARCHED STONE BRIDGE and follow the little path upstream. The valley narrows and, when you come to a METAL BRIDGE, Sass Corbee is just ahead. The river gushes through a steep, narrow gorge under an overhanging cliff, and it would be impossible to go further had not (precipitous) steps been cut into the huge fallen slab of limestone — **Sass Corbee** (**8**; **31min**). Return the same way.

Start Walk c by following Walk a to the PONTE NOGARA (**2**), and then continue along the river to join Walk b at **Chiodera** (**6**). Follow Walk b to **Sass Corbee** (**8**) and then keep walking upstream. The way is steep and a little vertiginous in places, but it is well marked with red dots and red/white stripes. You will have no difficulty route-finding if you keep to the left of the first ruin, to reach an open pasture. The deserted settlement of **Madri** (**9**) is poignant. Not many years ago this area was alive with people living and working here — now all you may see is a few cows.
Beyond Madri the path peters out completely, but simply follow the river until you come to a wooden footbridge. On the far side of the bridge the path goes downstream and then up and away from the river, to reach an asphalt road. Follow this to a junction near a small CHAPEL and turn left to descend to Naggio. Just after a modern house called LUCIA, take an old path down to the left that leads into **Naggio** itself. Turn right beside a water point and continue straight on to **San Antonio** church (**5**). Now follow Walk a from the 3h06min-point, to return to Piazza Camozzi in **Codogna** (**3**). If you are going on to Menaggio, walk along VIA 4 NOVEMBRE and follow the cobbled path down to the **Torrente Sanagra** (**2**), then retrace steps to **Menaggio** (**1**; **3h57min**).

Walk 13: MONTE GRONA (AND MONTE BREGAGNO)

Distance/time: 9.4km/5.8mi; 4h19min
Grade: ● ❢ strenuous. Mainly on well signposted and waymarked mountain paths, with an overall ascent/descent of 1000m/3280ft; you must be sure-footed and have a head for heights
Equipment: see page 26. Walking poles. Refreshments are available at Rifugio Menaggio in Jul/Aug and at weekends all year round.
Transport: 🚗 Leave Menaggio on the main road to Lugano and turn right after a few bends towards Plesio, beyond which is Breglia. Park near the bus stop (46° 3.202'N, 9° 14.054'E). 🚌 from Menaggio to Breglia; see 'Transport information' inside the back cover.
Nearest accommodation: Menaggio
Shorter walk: Rifugio Menaggio. 5.4km/3.4mi; 2h40min. ● Moderate, but with a steep ascent of 767m/2077ft. Equipment/access as above. Follow the main walk to the *rifugio* (6) and retrace steps.
Longer walk: Monte Bregagno. See page 70.

Climbing the steep mountain slopes to the craggy summit of Monte Grona is a challenge amply rewarded by stunning panoramic views. If you're here on a clear day, we highly recommend wandering on and up beyond San Amate towards Monte Bregagno on the superb flower-strewn ridge that follows.

Start the walk at the BUS STOP in **Breglia** (1): walk up the asphalt road and after about four minutes, take a path on the right to cut out a bend in the road; you cross a side road immediately. The route to the *rifugio* is clearly signposted and waymarked the whole way. Cross the main road when you meet it again, and climb to rejoin the road beside the bottom of the CABLE LIFT (2) to the Rifugio Menaggio. Turn left and, after a short way, signs indicate that you

leave the road and take a path to the left of a house, up between the other houses of **Monte Breglia**. Follow the waymarks and signs to rejoin the road, now a gravel track, and walk up to a BALCONY VIEWPOINT (3; **32min**) with picnic tables, a water tap and an information board.

Turn left here up a path. After about 20 you come to a WALKERS' PARKING AREA (usually choc-a-bloc) and then a bend with the first good views of Monte Grona and the *rifugio* below it. There are TWO ROUTES (4) from here to the *rifugio*, the lower (*basso*), and the higher *(alto)*, which we follow for the better views. Just after a sign pointing left to a water point, you reach another junction (5; **1h 10min**). The right-hand path leads to San Amate and Monte Bregagno and is our route of descent. Keep left, following the path as it contours the mountainside before the last short climb up to the **Rifugio Menaggio**, at a height of 1400m (6; **1h28min**). Enjoy a cappuccino and a bite to eat as you absorb the tremendous views from the terrace. Menaggio is below and the eastern arm of Lake Como stretches down towards Lecco. The interior of the *rifugio* is also very interesting, having a fine collection of photographs.

To continue, take the path from the rear of the *rifugio* that climbs to a junction just behind the helipad. Take the right fork, the 'VIA NORMALE', to Monte Grona. (The other marked routes are the *Via dirittissima*, steeper and harder, and the *Via ferrata*, which climbs on metal ladders). The 'normal' path climbs steadily up the steep grassy slopes that lie below the rocky ramparts of the mountain. Keep left at the next junction, to reach the little col of **Forcoletta** (7; **1h58min**).

Turn left and tackle the final climb to the summit. The way is across steep ground and the path, which divides into two (the upper is perhaps the finer route), may be vertiginous for some, but there is no technical difficulty. In contrast to the bare and rocky upper slopes on the south and east of Monte Grona (the routes taken by the other *vias*), these north slopes are wooded. Just before the summit you meet the *Via dirittissima*, which has climbed the steep southern slopes from the *rifugio*. A rocky scramble, with the assistance of a secure cable, now takes you up the last few metres to the SUMMIT of **Monte Grona** (8; **2h19min**), where you will find a cross and excellent viewpoint indicator. Your efforts are now rewarded by the view that encompasses a 360-degree panorama, including lakes Como and Lugano, and Monte Rosa on the western skyline. To the north is Monte Bregagno, beyond acres of upland pasture.

View east from the Rifugio Menaggio

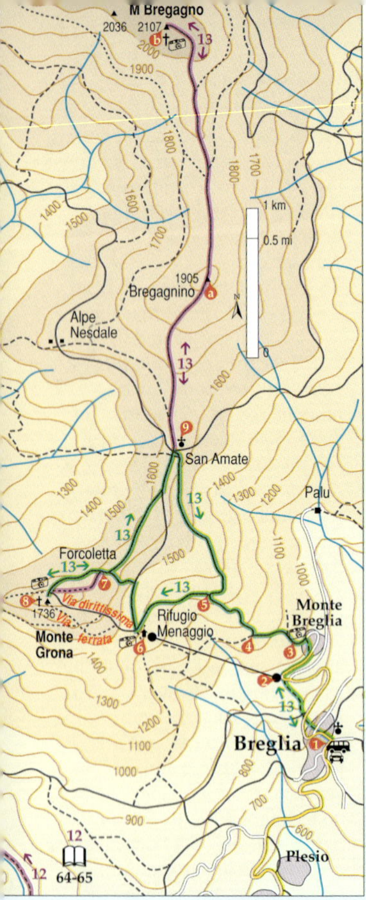

Retrace your steps to **Forcoletta**, and then walk along the beautiful grassy ridge. The music of cow bells resounds across the hillsides, and you may well meet the cow-herds who spend the summer at Alpe Nesdale. After about 13 minutes, ignore a path back down to the *rifugio* and, five minutes later, pass your return route to Breglia, just before you come to the little chapel of **San Amate** (**9**; **2h57min**). From here the main walk goes back to Breglia but, if you wish, you can continue along the ridge to Monte Bregagno (see Longer walk below).

To descend to Breglia follow the path off the ridge (eastwards), immediately forking to the right. The path descends easily, crossing the grassy slopes to reach a very large METAL BOARD. From here there is a good view across to Rifugio Menaggio and up to Monte Grona. Continue on to meet the junction first encountered at the 1h10min-point, from where you retrace your steps to **Breglia** (**4h19min**).

Longer walk: Monte Bregagno. 6.6km/4mi and a further 512m/ 1680ft of ascent; allow 2h30min. *Map and compass skills are necessary in mist.* From the chapel of **San Amate** continue along the wide grassy ridge. Climb to a top with a cairn (**Bregagnino, a**), reached in 35 minutes, and from here the route is clear. A cross marks the rounded SUMMIT of **Monte Bregagno** (**b**) — obviously a spot much-favoured by sheep! The views are wonderful: wave upon wave of mountains rise all around you, and much of Lake Como is visible. Retrace your steps to **San Amate** (**9**), then follow the main walk back to **Breglia** (**1**).

Rifugio Menaggio

Walk 14: MONTE GENEROSO

See also photograph on page 5

Distance/time: 8.7km/5.4mi; 2h29min

Grade: ● moderate; on good mountain paths and tracks, with 425m/1395ft of ascent/descent. Well signposted and waymarked

Equipment: see page 26. Refreshments are available at the Albergo Generoso.

Transport: 🚗 From Menaggio follow Car tour 3 through Lugano to Maroggia and then continue alongside Lake Lugano to Capolago, where clear signs direct you to the railway station and car park. Capolago can also be reached by ⛴ or 🚂 from Lugano. Take the cog railway to the Vetta station (Stazione Generoso Vetta). Train timetables vary, and you can pay in Swiss francs or euros. ***You will need your passport.***

Nearest accommodation: Lugano, Como

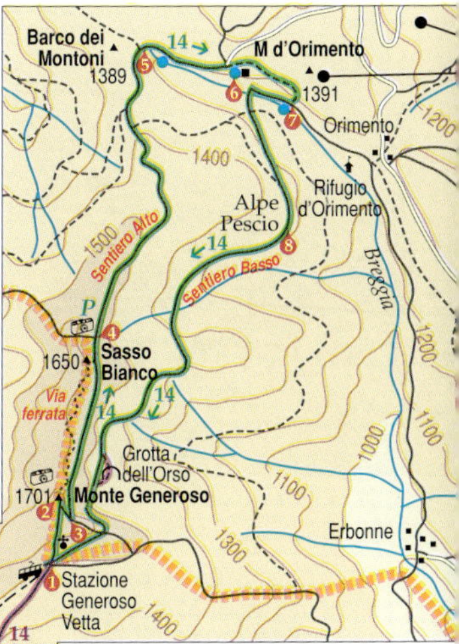

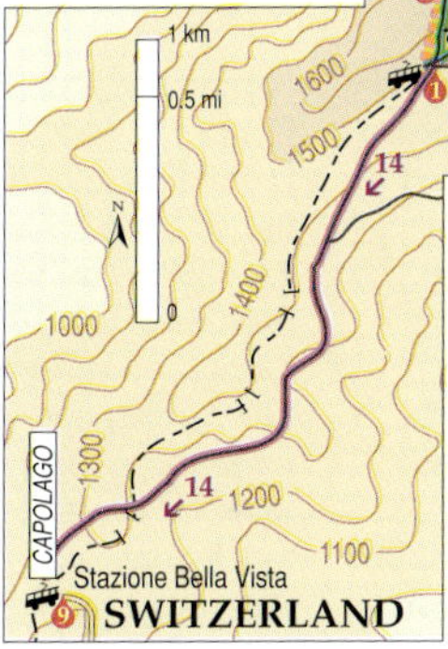

Short walk: Monte Generoso summit ridge. 3km/2mi; 1h20min. ● Easy, with ascents/ descents of about 300m/ 1000ft overall; equipment and access as above. Follow the main walk to the small GRASSY TOP just beyond the 34min-point (4) and then retrace your steps to the Stazione Generoso Vetta (1).

Alternative walk: Stazione Bella Vista. See page 72.

The steep ascent on the cog railway is just the start of this excellent day out on Monte Generoso, above Lake Lugano. Leaving behind the summit crowds, our route follows the mountain's crest and then returns by an easy traverse over the grassy eastern slopes. Here you may visit the cave famous for the remains found of the cave bear, which became extinct 18-20,000 years ago. (There are guided tours all day, but tickets must be pre-purchased at the restaurant by the Vetta station). Standing on the border between Italy and Switzerland, and with only smaller hills around, Monte Generoso affords far-reaching views on a clear day.

Start out from the **Stazione Generoso Vetta** platform (1): go up the flight of steps past the hotel and walk up beside a small CHAPEL, which has some colourful stained glass windows, following signs for VETTA GENEROSO. A wide path built of large limestone slabs

Picnic 7: view north from Monte Generoso to Lake Lugano

leads directly to the top, where the summit area of **Monte Generoso** (❷; **12min**) has been 'civilised' — a platform with protective railings and even a turnstile await you. The views are extensive — a magnificent 360-degree panorama. Viewpoint indicators help you pick out, on a clear day, distant mountains such as the Gran Paradiso, the Jungfrau, Mottarone and Monte Rosa, as well as parts of lakes Lugano, Maggiore and Como.

From the summit turnstile you *can* turn left and descend steeply to the path below, using a CABLE HANDRAIL. It is not difficult, but it may be too vertiginous for some. The easier route, which we recommend, is to retrace your steps for a few metres and then fork left along a path that follows the crest of the ridge. When you

Alternative walk: Descent to Stazione Bella Vista. 3km/2mi; 45min. ● Easy, with 400m/1300ft of descent. Equipment and access as main walk; return to Capolago from Stazione Bella Vista. This alternative can easily be added to the main walk or the Short walk. If you opt for this walk *only*, we do suggest that you first follow the main walk to the summit of Monte Generoso, to enjoy the spectacular views. **Start out** from the top of the flight of steps at the end of the **Stazione Generoso Vetta** (❶) platform: walk along a level path to a signposted junction. Turn right for BELLA VISTA, through a gate and down an asphalt path beside some buildings. Then turn left down a little ramp to find the beginning of a path that leads

Cog railway at Stazione Bella Vista, where refreshments are also available

across the open hillside below the railway. Along the way there are many panels with information about the mountain's flora, fauna and geology. The path is clearly signposted at the few junctions you meet and crosses the railway shortly before you reach **Stazione Bella Vista** (❾; **45min**).

meet a wire fence, walk left alongside it to a signposted junction, where you turn left for ORIMENTO (3). Follow this easy path along the side of the mountain, to come to a dip in the ridge almost immediately below the summit, and where the CABLE HANDRAIL mentioned above ends (**22min**). (From here you can easily climb to the next peak on the ridge. The view is as good as that from the main summit and, without the crowds, it is a fine place for a picnic. But *do not continue* along this ridge unless you have the necessary climbing equipment, knowledge, and confidence to tackle the *vias ferratas*.

Continue on the path below the grassy peak with lovely views across the alpine summer pastures. On the far side this top shows its true merit, displaying a series of rock towers and buttresses, and if you look carefully, you can see parts of the *via ferrata*. Continue on to a large SIGNPOST (4; **34min**), just before another GRASSY TOP on the ridge (Picnic 7). This is an excellent place to see the contrasting sides of Monte Generoso — the western face is steep, craggy and tree-covered, while the gently sloping eastern side is more open. *(The Short walk returns from here.)*

Turn right at this signpost to quickly meet the ridge again and descend to follow an old drystone wall, where you may see friendly ponies grazing. Trees now obscure the view to the west, but the eastern outlook more than compensates. At the next signpost turn left down into the trees on a rather eroded path and, after about six minutes, go right at another signpost. You now walk through shrubby birch woods until you come to a grassy area and a junction at **Barco dei Montoni** (5; **1h01min**), where there is a good map.

Turn right along a pleasant wide track, passing one small POND, to reach another POND BESIDE A BUILDING (6). Here the way is not obvious — you must turn right, through a gap in the fence, to enter a field next to the sign that points back to Monte Generoso. Keep left beside the fence, around the building, and then go through a further gap in the next fence, to join a wide grassy path. This descends easily across the open hillside. Above another POND you meet a track at a signpost (7; **1h18min**), where you turn right for MONTE GENEROSO SENTIERO BASSO (the 'lower route').

The track goes over a bridge across a small stream and then begins to climb through shrubby woodland, narrowing to a path. In about 15 minutes you leave the trees and can look back to Orimento, a small group of houses, with cattle grazing the surrounding slopes. The path rises steadily, passing old houses and buildings, many deserted. Just before a stream (most probably dry), turn right up some steps with a wooden handrail, to cross the same stream higher up. Now follow the path to a grassy ridge, the **Alpe Pescio** (8; **1h58min**), from where there is a good view back up to the summit of Monte Generoso.

A red arrow on a stone indicates the way from here, but the path is clear enough — it gradually climbs across the eastern slopes of the mountain. After about 18 minutes you will see a path that descends the short distance to the Grotta dell'Orso (Bear Cave). Unless you have an entrance ticket, continue up the final steep section, to gain the ridge (**2h23min**). Turn right here, to return along a fairly level path to the **Stazione Generoso Vetta** (1; **2h29min**).

Walk 15: CIRCUIT FROM ALPE DI LENNO

See also photographs on pages 2 and 5
Distance/time: 9.3km/5.8mi; 2h51min
Grade: ● easy-moderate; on good tracks and grassy mountain ridges, with approximately 410m/1345ft of ascent/descent
Equipment: see page 26. Good walking shoes will suffice. Refreshments are available from Rifugio Venini throughout Jul/Aug and at weekends from Mar to Dec.
Transport: 🚗 From Menaggio follow Car tour 3 in reverse to San Fedele Intelvi: drive south on the SS340 beside the lake Argegno and turn right in the village for 'Valle Intelvi'. Once in San Fedele, turn right in the centre and follow signs for Pigra, driving through the narrow streets of Blessagno. At Pigra bear left towards Alpe di Colonno, and continue on to the Rifugio Boffalora. Just after, at a fork in the road, bear right up to Alpe d'Ossuccio and follow the road to its end at Alpe di Lenno, where there is parking space (46° 0.322'N, 9° 9.198'E).
Nearest accommodation: San Fedele Intelvi, Lenno, Tremezzo
Short walk: Monte Calbiga. 3km/2mi; 1h02min. ● Easy; equipment and access as above. Follow the main walk to the **Rifugio Venini** (2) and, from the rear of this building, follow the main walk again from the 2h13min-point, to climb **Monte Calbiga** (8) and return to **Alpe di Lenno** (1).

This must be one of our favourite walks! You hike through flower-strewn summer pastures, with no strenuous climbing and with uninterrupted views. Choose a good day, take a picnic and revel in the magnificent mountain scenery.

Start out from **Alpe di Lenno** (1) and walk along the continuation of the road, now a gravel track. It rises gently and affords wonderful continuous views across Lake Como and down to Val Perlana and Ossuccio. Eventually you reach the **Rifugio Venini** (2; **24min**; Picnic 8), where there is a small WWI canon. *(The Short walk turns left here.)*

Continue on past the *rifugio*, ignoring the signpost for Sopra.

Pond near Alpe di Lenno

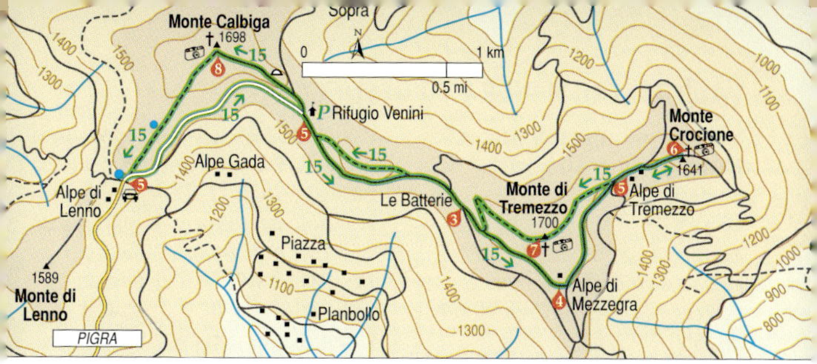

Extensive views open up all the time and, as you round a bend, you can see the two arms of Lake Como; down the steep hillside is the small church of San Benedetto. Soon, to the left of Monte di Tremezzo, Monte Crocione with its huge cross comes into sight. After about 15 minutes you reach a wide col, beyond which are some old WWI entrenchments. These rather elaborate stone built defences, **Le Batterie** (❸), never saw action.

Take the left-hand fork here, still on a track, and then, at a hairpin bend, go straight on through a METAL BARRIER. Continue on this track to reach **Alpe di Mezzegra** (❹; **55min**), a goat farm where you can buy butter and cheese in summer months.

Continue past the front of the buildings. Now follow a goats' path across the hillside on a gently rising traverse until you can see some ruins on a col ahead. A path leads down to these beautifully situated ruined buildings, **Alpe di Tremezzo** (❺). From here take the faint path along the ridge and climb the short slope to the SUMMIT of **Monte Crocione,** dominated by a large cross (❻; **1h18min**; photograph page 2). What a view! Nearly all of Lake Como is stretched out before you — the two southern arms of Lecco and Como and the northern part of the lake towards Colico. Below is Val Menaggio, Lake Piano and the villages visited on Walk 12; above these is Monte Grona (Walk 13). Numerous other mountain peaks can also be seen, so it is a great place to get your bearings.

To return you *could* retrace your steps, but we recommend a slightly more strenuous ridge walk all the way back to Alpe di Lenno. By doing this you can enjoy panoramic vistas the whole time. Return to **Alpe di Tremezzo** (❺) and then climb the ridge ahead to the SUMMIT of **Monte di Tremezzo** (❼; **1h39min**), marked by a modern bronze Madonna with an ice axe and rope beneath.

Now keep on along the ridge back to **Le Batterie** (❸) and continue over a series of small rises on the crest of the ridge, before dropping down to the **Rifugio Venini** (❷; **2h13min**).

From the rear of the *rifugio* follow a track up past an OBSERVATORY and, soon after, take a path that climbs steeply to the SUMMIT of **Monte Calbiga** (❽; **2h29min**). Crowning this summit is a modern cross and various items of metal artwork. From here you enjoy a different, but equally wonderful view down onto Lake Lugano and beyond, in the far distance, you can even see Lake Maggiore.

The way forward is now along the ridge in the direction of the distant, but very distinct, Monte Generoso (Walk 14). Descend quite steeply to a small POND and then continue along the ridge before finally dropping down to the rather larger POND at **Alpe di Lenno** (❶; **2h51min**).

Walk 16: FROM PIGRA TO OSSUCCIO

See also photograph page 30
Distance/time: 10.8km/6.7mi; 3h30min
Grade: strenuous, with steep ascents of 350m/1150ft overall and an incredibly steep final descent of approximately 800m/2625ft
Equipment: see page 26. Walking poles. Refreshments are available at the Santuario della Madonna.
Transport: from Menaggio towards Como (see 'Transport information' inside the back cover); alight at the cable car in Argegno. Take this to Pigra. When you arrive at Ossuccio, use the same service to return to Menaggio.
Nearest accommodation: San Fedele Intelvi, Lenno, Tremezzo
Short walk: Santuario della Madonna del Soccorso from Ossuccio. 2.6km/1.6mi; allow an hour. Easy; a short but steep ascent/descent of 200m/650ft; equipment as above. Access: or to the post office in Ossuccio (45° 58.061'N, 9° 11.105'E). **Start out** at the BUS STOP (9): walk along the busy main road towards Como for a few metres, then go up behind the church of **Santa Eufemia**. You meet an asphalt road that you follow straight uphill until you come to a restaurant, LOCANDA GARZOLA. Go left and then go right immediately, again uphill. When you reach CHAPEL NO. 4, follow the cobbled walkway up past more numbered chapels, to the **Santuario della Madonna del Soccorso** (8). Return by retracing your steps to **Ossuccio** (**1h**).

Strong legs are needed on this walk, as it involves a steep ascent and an even steeper descent. However your efforts are more than worthwhile. You visit delightful, quiet mountain villages and walk through farmland amidst belled cows and horses, with breathtaking views of Lake Como.

Start out at the CABLE CAR STATION at **Pigra** (1): walk up the road into the village, passing several bars. Go straight ahead at the roundabout, continuing up through the attractive houses and colourful gardens. When you reach the POST OFFICE and LIBRARY, take the narrow asphalt road uphill to the left (*not* the cobbled road). At the next junction, by the WASHHOUSE, turn right. When the road ends by a large building ('Societa Operaia'), keep right on a much narrower road signposted 'STRADA LOMIA — CORNIGA' (**8min**).

This road soon becomes a track and descends through trees. Shortly after passing a large water trough and crossing a small stream, bear right at a fork that is signposted to CORNIGA. The track descends again, reduces to a path and crosses two more stream beds (most likely dry); at the second of these you will see 'SERTA' and an arrow painted on rocks. From here you rise steeply to a small collec-

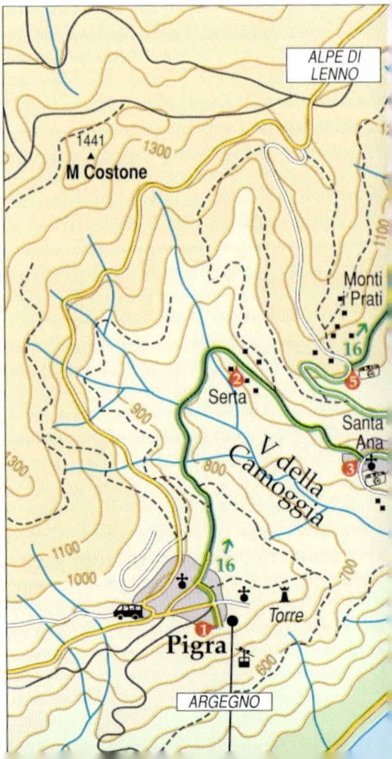

tion of houses, **Serta** (**2**; **35min**). Walk by the houses and then drop gently on the wooded path, following some blue paint marks, to come to **Corniga** (**3**; **51min**). This attractive little village sits opposite Pigra across the tree-filled valley. Follow the path to the small church of **Santa Anna**, built in 1631, from where there is an excellent view. Take the track at the left-hand side of the church (red paint waymarks); this rises very steeply out of the village. Huff and puff up to the hamlet of **Solasco** (**4**), to be rewarded with your first good view of Lake Como. Above the houses the old track, which is amazingly steep, climbs again through woodland. You will be pleased to see the first houses of **Monti i Prati** (**1h 36min**). Enjoy the ever-improving views as you walk up past the houses, but ***watch for your next turning*** (**5**), a grassy track to the

Near Gravona: view over Lenno and Lake Como to Bellagio

Santuario della Madonna del Soccorso, above Ossuccio

right — beside a wall where 'BAITA CARLIN TITAL' (the name of a farmhouse) is faintly inscribed in red. (If you reach a concrete road that climbs up by a row of small houses you have missed the turning; retrace your steps just a few metres).

Once you've turned right your steep ascent is over! The grassy track leads down to the farmhouse. Walk around the front of it and take the path that runs across the hillside alongside a fence, with views to the far side of Lake Como. You pass in front of more houses and then descend through an avenue of trees and woodland, to a small stream. After crossing you emerge on open pasture by the hamlet of Canelva — a wonderful spot for a picnic with lovely open views.

In **Canelva** (6; **2h05min**) you come to an important junction by the few remaining ruins of a house. Follow the fingerpost on the house opposite, pointing left uphill to COLOMBERA. Then, after about 50m, take a path between the houses on the right (another fingerpost).

Follow this narrow path, which becomes tree-lined and goes through a gate. After about 13 minutes you reach more buildings and then pasture again; from here Bellagio looks like a jewel in the centre of Lake Como. The way continues past a SPRING where you can replenish your water and, less than a minute later, you come to a junction in the area of **Gravona** (7; **2h26min**).

Keep right here, to begin a knee-crunching descent on an old mule track — now concreted for car use by brave drivers! (After about 32 minutes a signpost indicates a route up Val Perlana to the little church that you can see on the wooded hillside, San Benedetto, which dates from the late 11th century). This long descent has fantastic views across the red-roofed villages and towns down to the lake.

In another eight minutes you reach the **Santuario della Madonna del Soccorso** (8; **3h06min**). Behind it is a bar/trattoria and picnic tables. Look for the appealing shrine set in the hollow of a plane tree (see page 30). From the balcony of the church follow the wide cobbled walkway down past a series of fascinating 17th-century chapels, containing life-size statutes and graphic paintings, each depicting a significant chapter in the life of Christ. At CHAPEL NO. 4 the cobbled way ends; keep straight on towards the lake, to reach a restaurant, LOCANDA GARZOLA. Go left here and then immediately right, down the straight road. The road bends left to the church of **Santa Eufemia**. Keep to the left of the church and meet the busy main road, where you turn left to the POST OFFICE and BUS STOP in **Ossuccio** (9; **3h30min**).

Walk 17: SAN MARTINO AND IL DOSSONE

Distance/time: 9.7km/6mi; 3h29min
Grade: ● moderate, on good paths and tracks; ascent of 700m/2300ft; easy route-finding despite sparse signposting/waymarking
Equipment: see page 26. Walking poles. Refreshments are available at Griante and Croce.
Transport: 🚌 from Menaggio to Griante (see 'Transport information' inside the back cover); alight at the Hotel Brittania Excelsior. Or ⛴ from Menaggio to Cadenabbia, then walk a short way north to the Hotel Brittania Excelsior. Return on 🚌 from Croce to Menaggio, or walk back (2km/1.2mi; +28min; see page 81)
Nearest accommodation: Menaggio or Tremezzo
Short Walk: San Martino. 3.8km/2.4mi; 1h45min. ● Easy; ascent of 300m/1000ft; equipment as main walk. Transport: 🚗 to Griante, 3km south of Menaggio; park by San Rocco church (45° 59.819'N, 9° 13.953'E). Follow the main walk to **San Martino** (3) and return the same way.

From the shore of Lake Como you may see tiny white churches perched high on the hillsides. On this walk we take you up to one of them, but then continue up steep cliffs to a scenic hilltop. It would be easy to spend a whole day here, savouring the views.

Start at the HOTEL BRITTANIA EXCELSIOR (1) in **Griante**. Walk up the road on the right-hand side of the hotel for a short way, then take the steps that climb up from the first bend (where there is a CHURCH on your left). At the top of the steps turn right along VIA G BRENTANO, to come to a junction by a WAR MEMORIAL, where you turn left past a TENNIS COURT. As you walk along you will spot the little church of San Martino, high on the cliffs to your right. At a T-junction, turn right down the attractive PASSEGGIATA ADENAUER,

which goes under an archway with a house on top and then becomes pedestrianised. Turn left at the end of this street (signposted to SAN MARTINO), soon coming to the small frescoed church of **San Rocco** in a *piazza* of the same name (❷; **16min**).

From the rear of this small square take the well-signposted narrow asphalt road (VIA SAN MARTINO). Follow signs for SAN MARTINO, heading right down a few steps to cross a bridge over a usually dry stream bed. After passing a well-kept SHRINE, the cobbled mule track rises gently, winding up past old farms, with little SHRINES marking your progress. Ignore a path off to the right and continue up to a poignant WAR MEMORIAL (**41min**), built by the local mountaineering club in 1977. Paintings on the wall vividly depict the fact that the soldiers suffered as much from the terrible mountain conditions as from the hands of their enemies. Seats nearby look out across the lake.

From here continue up through an avenue of trees for seven minutes, until you reach a junction from where you can just see the top of the church. Turn right here along the path with the hand railing and cross the upland pasture, grazed by inquisitive goats. Note the path on the left, just before the 'Beware Falling Rocks' sign; this is your onward route). Pass a SPRING and soon reach a gate (please close it behind you, as requested by the signs), then come to **San Martino** (❸; **57min**). The church perches on a grassy shelf with steep limestone cliffs above and below — you feel you are standing on an eagle's eyrie! There are tremendous views over Lake Como, especially across to Bellagio and over most of Lago di Lecco.

Retrace your steps to the junction beside the 'BEWARE FALLING ROCKS' SIGN. Turn right on a narrow path, which contours the mountainside and quickly reaches a small house (**1h07min**). Continue along beside the metal railings and then keep right at a fork, to start climbing in a series of zigzags. The path is well graded, working its way up the steep cliffs, and is mostly on the open hillside with lovely vistas. Looking back there is a picture-postcard view of San Martino, which superbly shows its high and isolated position. The path is eroded higher up but is easy enough to follow up to a summer pasture below the few houses of **Pilone**. It continues to zigzag across to the houses, which nestle just below the summit of **Sasso di San Martino** (❹; **2h04min**).

Your route goes in front and to the left of two of these buildings, through a small wooded area where you keep to the left on the main path (signposted). Soon, climb once more on the open hillside in a series of easy zigzags that end abruptly at a little GRASSY COL. (Directly ahead is the huge bulk of Monte Crocione, one of the vantage points on Walk 15.) Turn right here, to go past a pylon and up to the SUMMIT of **Il Dossone** (❺; **2h26min**). This is a superb spot for a picnic with a birds-eye view down to the Val Menaggio and the villages of Naggio and Codogna, visited on Walk 12. The views to the east are no less impressive, with the Grigna range dominating the skyline above the eastern shore of Lake Como.

Rested, now return to the GRASSY COL and turn right along the wide path that descends into the trees. Keep on the main path, where you may see the odd red waymark, until you reach a junction beside a charming SHRINE at **Bocchetta di**

Nava (6; 2h39min). Bear right, now on a motorable track, and quickly pass some summer houses. You will see a **'NO. 2'** waymark that indicates that you are on the long-distance path, the **Via Monti Lariani** (a seven-day walk from Cernobbio to Sorico). Continue down this road through the trees, ignoring a blue arrow on a building after about 15 minutes, and walk through an area called **Mie**. Go through a road barrier and soon meet an asphalt road near the chapel of **Madonna di Paullo** (7; **3h12min**).

Turn right here, after about eight minutes passing the entrance to a GOLF COURSE, and descend into **Croce**. Just after house No. 50, short-cut a bend in the road by taking a path on your left. Cross the road at the bottom by a large PYLON, to cut out another bend. Continue on the wide asphalt road beside new houses and, just opposite No. 27, descend some waymarked steps on your left that double back the way you came. Then follow the path to meet the road once more. Now turn left, past the WASHHOUSE, to join the main road near the CHURCH (8; **3h29min**). The BUS STOP is just beyond this church on the main road.

If you miss the bus, walk back to Menaggio: take the cobbled path

Above: San Martino; left: goat near the church

near the bus stop (VIA V CASARTELLI). This leads down to the HOSPITAL, where you walk out of the main vehicle entrance to rejoin the main road. Head down the road to the first right-hand hairpin bend where, on the far side, you can cut out a bend by descending some steps. Cross straight over by the entrance sign to Menaggio and walk down the road opposite (VIA MONTI GRAPPA), until you meet the main road again. Cross over and follow the sign for the LOVENO HOTEL, down another road. After about 50m turn right to follow a cobbled road, past the church of **San Carlo** and down under an ARCHWAY. Ignore any turnings until you come to a T-junction, where you turn right and then take the next left beside **San Stefano**. Cross the busy road in front of the church and walk down VIA CALVI to the Piazza Garibaldi in the centre of **Menaggio** (9; **3h57min**).

Walk 18: ALPE DI MEZZO AND MONTE BERLINGHERA

Distance/time: 13.3km/8.2mi; 3h58min
Grade: ● moderate-strenuous; mainly on good — but not always waymarked — tracks and paths, with an overall ascent/descent of approximately 650m/2130ft
Equipment: see page 26. Walking poles. No refreshments available en route.
Transport: 🚗 From Menaggio follow the lakeside road north towards Colico as far as Val di Gera (23.5km/14.5mi), where you cross the bridge and turn left towards Montemezzo. Fork right to Bugiallo and then follow this twisting road up to and through Fordeccia. After the road levels out, with stunning views southwards, turn right at an *unsignposted* junction to the church of San Bartolomeo just above, where you can park (46° 11.605'N, 9° 23.145'E).
Nearest accommodation: Menaggio, Gravedona
Shorter walk: Monte Berlinghera. 7.7km/4.8mi; 3h. ● Grade, equipment and access as above (overall ascent/descent 700m/2300ft. See notes on facing page. If you wish to combine this walk with the main walk, on the return from Berlinghera do *not* turn left at the junction between the *alpes* of Mezzo and Pescedo towards (❷). Instead continue straight on, ford a small stream and then fork right, to pass behind the houses of Alpe di Mezzo on a bulldozed track and join the main walk just after the 45min-point, by the SHRINE.

On this high-level walk there are several options, depending on the amount of time and energy you have. A short hike will take you to the tranquil *alpes* of Mezzo and Pescedo, and just above is Bocchetta di Chiaro, from where there are wonderful views. With only a little more exertion, you can reach Monte Berlinghera. The Shorter walk and the main walk can be easily combined, and we would recommend this for the outstanding, ever-changing vistas and the elation felt from a fulfilling day in the hills.

The walk starts at **San Bartolomeo** (❶), which looks more like a house than a church. From here you already have an idea of the views in store on this walk. Opposite is a signposted path to SASSO CANALE. Take this, climbing through the pine trees and past a few houses. Beyond the last house, in a level grassy area, the path goes left into the trees once more. Waymarks are few and far between, but continue upwards and to the left to reach a wide track (**15min**).

Turn left, and after a further steep climb, keep straight ahead on a rough, stony track (where the main track bends to the right). In another seven minutes you rejoin the main track, behind a small building. Turn left here and soon, through a wide gap in the trees, you have a superb view that encompasses Monte Grona, Monte di Tremezzo and Menaggio. Go under an electricity line and around a bend, to leave the trees behind. You now enter the *alpes* of Mezzo on the left and Pescedo on the right — tiny settlements on the open hillsides (**37min**). There is an attractive water point here, shown overleaf, beside a signpost and some picnic tables.

Continue up the track and then TURN LEFT (❷), following the waymarks, towards the houses of **Alpe di Mezzo** (**45min**). Walk to the right of these buildings and

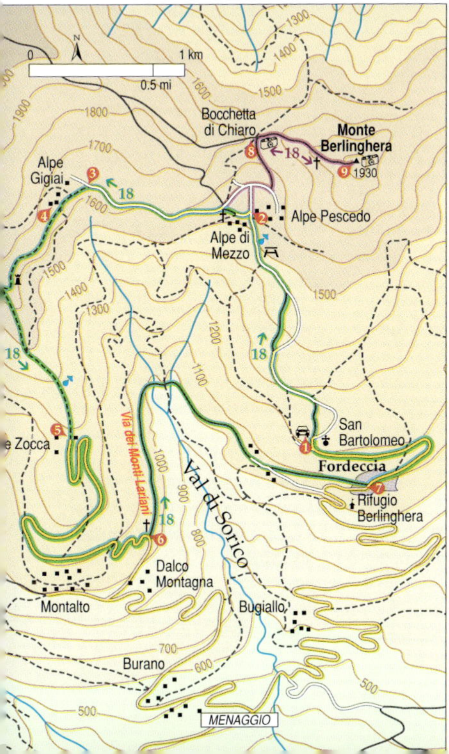

Shorter walk: Follow the main walk to the 37min-point. Then do *not* turn left towards the houses of Alpe di Mezzo; instead, *leave* the waymarks and continue up the track to a T-junction. Turn right and, where the track bends towards Alpe Pescedo, take a track to the left. Pass a tiny stone building and, at a tall lone pine tree, leave the track and climb a faint grassy path on the right. This joins another, clearer path, where you turn left and climb to a large pylon at the pass of **Bocchetta di Chiaro** (8) Go right here, towards the trees, and follow the zigzag path up through rhododendrons and shrubby pines, gaining the ridge by a CROSS. The final climb is ahead and clearly visible. It is steep near the top and you will need to pick your own route over the rocky slopes. Awaiting you at the SUMMIT of **Monte Berlinghera** (9; **1h 37min**) is a panorama encompassing Lake Como, Sasso Canale to the west, the Chiavenna range and the steep rugged peaks above Lago di Mezzola. Return by retracing your steps to **San Bartolomeo** (1; **3h**).

Photograph: View east from Monte Berlinghera (Shorter walk)

Attractively carved water point at Alpe di Mezzo

follow the waymarks up to a small white SHRINE. Just above is a bulldozed track where you turn left, leaving the waymarks and enjoying marvellous views down Lake Como as you go. Pass through an old drystone wall that continues up to the ridge on your right; you can see Alpe Gigiai ahead. Follow the track until it turns to the right and starts to climb. At this point take a SMALL PATH THAT GOES LEFT (3), fording a stream and traversing the slopes to **Alpe Gigiai** (4; **1h08min**), which consists of a few farm buildings, mostly ruined, but some still in use.

From here three paths lead onward. The upper path ascends steeply on the mountainside, the lower path drops gently and contours above Val di Sorico. To find the centre path — your ongoing route — start from the front of the last intact building and walk in front of three that are in ruins. After a few metres, pick up the path that climbs at a gentle angle towards the ridge ahead. Enjoy the superb views, especially back to Monte Berlinghera and the *alpes* of Mezzo and Pescedo. You come to a small MEMORIAL and, just after, gain the crest of the ridge that falls steeply from the mountaintop (**1h27min**).

Turn left along a faint path down the ridge. Below you is Alpe Zocca and the end of an asphalt road — your next objective. Just before you enter the trees, the path leaves the crest of the ridge and drops steeply to the right, to a small house with a picnic table and water trough nearby. Continue across a grassy area to reach the rough track that leads to **Alpe Zocca** (5; **1h57min**). Here keep straight ahead, to come to the end of the asphalt road.

Follow the road as it winds its way down the end of the broad ridge, with fine views across Lake Como. The road overlooks the houses of **Montalto**, and on the hillside opposite is the white church of San Bartolomeo, prominent above the village of Fordeccia. Eventually you reach some houses by a series of bends. It is possible to avoid a few of these hairpins by taking short cuts down the grassy slopes, but *be careful not to miss the bend where you turn left off the road.* This is marked by a small SHRINE and a signpost indicating the long distance footpath, the VIA DEI MONTI LARIANI (6; **2h30min**).

Take this waymarked route that contours around the steep-sided **Val di Sorico** through attractive birch woods, the path becoming narrow near the head of the valley. After 22 minutes you cross a stream and five minutes later you cross another. The path now climbs steeply for a short time, before levelling off to reach a grassy *alpe* and a few houses (**3h17min**).

Continue along a track past more houses and then, after about seven minutes, look for the waymarked path that leads to the left. This path climbs easily through the trees up to the village of **Fordeccia,** where you may see foraging goats and pigs. The waymarks take you through the houses to the ROAD (7; **3h31min**), from where you follow the route you drove earlier to return to **San Bartolomeo** (**3h58min**).

Walk 19: SENTIERO DEL VIANDANTE

Distance/time: 5.4km/3.3mi; 1h13min
Grade: ● easy; well signposted and waymarked, with ups and downs of 200m/650ft overall
Equipment: see page 26. Trainers will suffice. Refreshments are available in Bellano and Varenna.
Transport: ⛴ to Bellano or by 🚗 (a detour on Car tour 4): park in Bellano nearest parking is south of the river (46° 2.445'N, 9° 18.174'E). Return by ferry to your resort or to Bellano to collect your car
Nearest accommodation: Menaggio, Bellagio, Bellano or Varenna

On this walk we take you along part of the long-distance footpath, the Sentiero del Viandante, which runs above the lakeside villages from just north of Lecco to near Colico. We explore the section that links Bellano, famous for its gorges, with Varenna, an old medieval town with a pretty square and narrow cobbled streets. We describe the route from Bellano to Varenna, but the route can easily be reversed (see notes on page 86). To top it all you can enjoy a lovely, relaxing ferry ride back to your resort.

Start out from the FERRY TERMINAL in **Bellano** (❶). Cross the very busy main road opposite and go through an archway, along a short cobbled walkway. Turn right at the end and then bear right to return to the main road (or bear left if you want to go to the tourist information office first). Turn left on the main road and, after crossing the river, take the first turn left, signposted to VALSASSINA. Follow this road around to the left and across the RAILWAY LINE. You now climb until, beside a zebra crossing, you turn left up some cobbled steps. At the top — back on the Valsassina road, turn left. But cross the road after just a few metres, to find the start of a signposted path to RIVALBA (**13min**) — part of the **Sentiero del Viandante**.

Walk along this cobbled path that quickly climbs above the town. There are now good views across to Menaggio on the far side of Lake Como, and to Monte di Tremezzo (Walk 15), an easily recognisable mountain because of the diagonal lines of white cliffs on its thickly wooded slopes. You are above old houses with steep but still-used terraces, some with vines while others have orchards and vegetables.

When you reach a small chapel, the **Cappella dell'Addolorata** (❷; **26min**), carry on to cross a wooden BRIDGE. Shortly after, you come to a large building called LA FABRICA (❸). Continue straight ahead here, with more splendid

Varenna (top) and Bellano (bottom)

views back towards the head of Lake Como and down to Bellano and Dervio. Wild flowers cloak the old terraces and cover the verges. You pass a ruined SHRINE and cross an old BRIDGE over the *funivia* that once serviced **Regoledo** (4; **39min**), the village just above. No longer used, it is quickly being reclaimed by nature.

After the bridge, ignore a stepped path to the left and climb gently once more, before descending by terraces filled with olive trees. At a pink SHRINE you can see the unspoilt village of Gittana across the little valley and, somewhere below, traffic is speeding along the *autostrada* that tunnels through the hillside. Continue on to cross a BRIDGE by a small water shoot and walk above **Gittana**. About four minutes later a path joins from the left, beyond which the way forks. Keep left uphill here; pass another old SHRINE and meet an asphalt road at a junction (**50min**). Walk up the road opposite towards PERLEDO), to a renovated CHAPEL (5). Ignore a path to the right just past the chapel, but a few metres/yards further on, turn down right through woods on a steep cobbled mule trail. This ends by the drive to house No. 11. Follow this downhill, with glimpses over Varenna and to the Bellagio peninsula beyond.

At the end of the drive you reach a busy main road. Turn right downhill and, just around the first bend, by house No. 29, take the stepped path that runs between high walls. Cross the main road three times, continuing your descent. The path eventually becomes a narrow asphalt road before joining the main road again opposite the RAILWAY STATION. Turn left here. A path cuts out the last short bend before you go under the RAILWAY BRIDGE. From here follow the road down to the lakeside road through **Varenna**. Go straight over and follow the river, which you cross by an attractive little footbridge, to walk along the front and on to the FERRY TERMINAL (6; **1h13min**).

The route in reverse: From the FERRY TERMINAL in **Varenna** (6) turn left along the front to cross the river. Walk up to the main road, cross it, and follow the road opposite towards ESINO LARIO. Go under the RAILWAY and, a little way up the road, turn right uphill on a narrow asphalt road by house No. 1. This road becomes a cobbled path. You cross the main road three times and then follow it to the left, to reach the **Sentiero del Viandante**, which is clearly signposted all the way from here to **Bellano**.

Walk 20: GRIGNA SETTENTRIONALE

Distance/time: 12km/7.4mi; 5h47min.
Grade: ●⁚⁚ very strenuous, with about 1000m/3280ft of ascent/descent. You must be sure-footed and have a head for heights. This is a serious mountain walk suitable only for those with experience. Snow can linger on the approach over the northern slopes well into June and return as early as September. There are several sections where chains or cables are provided: those nearer the summit are a necessity — the route would be impossible without them (except for rock climbers). ***Be prepared to turn back and remember that you have to return down the top two cable sections.***
Equipment: see page 26. Walking poles. Refreshments are available on the summit of Grigna Settentrionale from Rifugio Luigi Brioschi, which is open all year and, in season, from the other *rifugios* en route.
Transport: 🚗 From Varenna follow Car tour 4 to the far side of Esino Lario. Above the village turn right to reach the skiing area and *rifugio* at Cainallo. Fork left here and continue up the narrowing road to its end at Vo di Moncodeno, where there is parking (45° 58.812'N, 9° 21.772'E).
Nearest accommodation: Menaggio, Bellagio, Bellano or Varenna
Short walk: Porta Prada. 3.8km/2.4mi; 1h29min. ● Easy ascent/descent of about 225m/740ft; trainers will suffice; access as above. Follow the main walk as far as the rock arch, **Porta Prada** (4; 49min) and return the same way.

Grigna is one of the highest mountains around Lake Como. It has two separate peaks, the northern (settentrionale) and southern (meridionale). Although this walk starts at over 1400m/4593ft, it is still a strenuous and demanding undertaking to reach our objective — the higher, northern summit. We follow a route that not only includes some interesting features, but also gives an appreciation of the immensity and grandeur of this special mountain.

Start out at the PARKING AREA at **Vo di Moncodeno** (1): walk up the grassy slope towards the skyline, seen through a wide break in the trees, to find a signpost. You will follow ROUTE 24, to BIETTI. The clear path climbs through woodland to a little SHRINE from where you can see your goal, the summit of Grigna, over the deep and densely wooded **Valle dei Molini**. You can now begin to appreciate the size and scale of this mountain. Continue on, traversing through beech woods around the headwall of the valley, gently climbing.

At a junction (**33min**), turn steeply right uphill on a badly eroded path, to reach a col, the **Bocchetta di Prada** (2). Turn left here, still on ROUTE 24, to come to a small chapel, **Cappella Votiva** (3; **41min**; Picnic 9), which overlooks **Valle di Era** leading down to Lake Como.

From here ROUTE 24 bears right, quickly reaching the amazing natural rock arch shown on page 89, the **Porta Prada** (4; **49min**; another setting for Picnic 9). It is possible to go under the arch, which has a crucifix set in it, but you must return to the main path to continue. *(The Short walk turns back here.)* The main path runs to the left of the arch and traverses

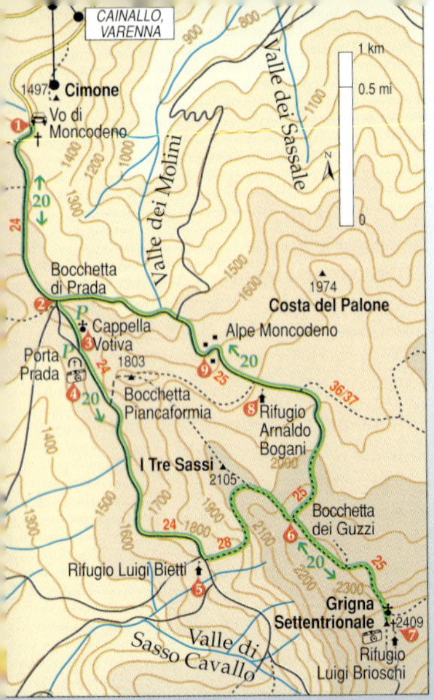

under the long northwest ridge of the mountain. To the west you can now see, in the far distance, the huge bulk of Monte Rosa. You pass a route that climbs up to the ridge and, soon after, the path loses height in a series of zigzags to cross a rocky GULLY (**1h07min**). The waymarking, especially the yellow arrows on the next short section, can be a bit confusing. Climb out of the gully and bear right at a junction; a little further on, *ignore* the yellow arrows and keep to the right. In about 10 minutes you go through a gate from where you can see the town of Mandello del Lario below, on the shores of the Lecco arm of Lake Como. The way is now easy to follow as it traverses the mountainside to **Rifugio Luigi Bietti** (**5**; **1h33min**). The *rifugio* is beautifully sited on a grassy shelf beneath the western wall of Grigna Settentrionale. Walk to a signpost at the rear of the *rifugio,* beside the woodpiles.

You now take ROUTE 28, 'RIFUGIO BRIOSCHI VIA GUZZI' — a steep, strenuous ascent that begins up a wide grassy spur heading for the rocky towers above. Yellow paint marks, few at first, guide you clearly up to the ridge. The final section is an easy scramble over the rocky slopes, with two short lengths of chain to help you up. You reach the ridge at **Bocchetta dei Guzzi** (**6**; **2h24min**), overlooking the rocky corrie through which you will later descend.

Turn right along the ridge towards the (still-hidden) summit. Rather than follow the crest, the path keeps to its left. After about five minutes you regain the ridge and can see the summit — still a long way off. Negotiate a little step and follow the yellow waymarks across the steep rocky slopes, leaving the crest once more, to drop down to a clear path (**2h50min**). Now follow ROUTE 25, signposted to the RIFUGIO BRIOSCHI.

In about six minutes you reach the FIRST OF THE TWO CABLED SECTIONS. This one helps you make a rising traverse across a rocky ledge, presents no difficulty,

Rifugio Luigi Brioschi on Grigna Settentrionale

and is not vertiginous. Continue up the stony path to the SECOND CABLE that ascends *very steeply and is much more difficult and strenuous.* The cable is at waist height, and we tackled it by leaning back and pulling ourselves along, with our feet walking up the rocks — a bit like abseiling, but in reverse! Some people may find this vertiginous and ***remember that you also have to descend this way.***

Beyond the cable it is a simple walk, past an unusual modern CHAPEL built in glass, to reach the **Rifugio Luigi Brioschi** (7; **3h20min**), just below the SUMMIT CROSS of **Grigna Settentrionale**. What a panorama awaits you! Mountains, mountains and more mountains. Southwards is the rugged-looking Grigna Meridionale and below the green valley of Valsassina. The Matterhorn and Monte Rosa are easily identified, and all of the summits climbed in the walks on Car tour 3 are clearly visible. Enjoy some refreshment at the *rifugio,* and prepare yourselves for the descent.

Return down the CABLES to the junction you first met at the 2h50min-point (**3h45min**) and bear right for RIFUGIO BOGANI and CAINALLO (still ROUTE 25). *Care is needed* on the next part of the descent, which is steep and rugged but not difficult. A yellow sign a few metres down warns you of *danger*. The path circles above a huge and seemingly bottomless PIT, ***beware!*** — the two memorials here are a sobering reminder. There are more PITS, SINKHOLES and GULLIES along the way, and there is one short section where a CHAIN is provided for assistance. (The high metal poles with silver discs indicate, we think, a safe winter route avoiding all the pits).

Eventually the gradient eases and the terrain becomes less rocky with more grass and a few shrubby pines. Skirt to the left of a large grassy bowl and stay above the floor of the valley that runs away

Porta Prada (Picnic 9)

from it. There are a myriad of paths in this area; if you find yourselves on ROUTES 36 AND 37, follow them to the left, to reach a signpost just above a *rifugio*. Walk downhill from this point to the attractive **Rifugio Arnaldo Bogani** (8; **4h40min**).

From here you still follow ROUTE 25, now signposted to ESINO and CAINALLO. You quickly come to another junction where you bear right and continue down the grassy hillside and past the buildings of **Alpe Moncodeno** (9), where you may see goats and pigs. The path now drops steeply through pine trees and, after passing a path off to the right, goes through a gate. You then traverse the steep headwall of **Valle dei Molini**, with sheer limestone cliffs above and, across the valley, a magnificent rock tower. In several places the path has been shored up with pine logs, but there is no danger. Climb a short way to reach the junction you first met at the 33min-point (below the Bocchetta di Prada), and then retrace your steps to **Vo di Moncodeno** (1; **5h47min**).

Walk 21: CAPPELLA AND CHIESA SAN MARTINO

Distance/time: 7km/4.3mi; 2h24min

Grade: ● moderate; on good waymarked and signposted paths, with about 320m/1050ft of ascent

Equipment: see page 26. Walking poles. Refreshments are available, in season, from the *rifugio* at Chiesa San Martino.

Transport: 🚗 Follow Car tour 4. Approaching Laorca en route to Lecco, you pass under a large sign, 'Lecco'. Some 300m further on, the road makes a hairpin bend to the left. Turn up right off the road here (*not* signposted when last checked). Follow this road around to the left and park where it ends, at the rear of Laorca (45° 52.856'N, 9° 24.385'E). If coming directly from Bellagio, cross the *second* bridge over the river Adda into Lecco, following signs for Valsassina. Keep right at the first roundabout and then straight on, to go under the railway bridge. At an oddly shaped junction follow Valsassina again, going left and then right. Laorca has no sign but, when you have left the narrow streets behind, look for an IVECO *autoparazioni* (service station) — on your left on a wide left-hand bend. Just beyond it, the road hairpins to the right. Turn left off the hairpin (*not* signposted when last checked). Follow the road and park as above. 🚌 from Lecco to Laorca (see 'Transport information' inside the back cover). From the bus stop, cross the road and climb the steps. Turn right at the top and then left by a sign for Val Caloden. Soon bear right, ignoring a left turn, and then quickly take the next turn, sharp left, up to the piazza in front of the church. From here follow the main walk from the 1min-point. Return on 🚌 from Laorca to Lecco.

Nearest accommodation: Lecco, Bellagio, Varenna or Bellano

This short walk takes you to an attractive hillside chapel, seldom visited by tourists, but a popular route for climbers tackling the *vias ferratas* on the steep cliffs of Corno Medale. From the balcony there is a bird's-eye view down to Lecco, situated at the end of Lake Como, and across to the craggy limestone cliffs of Resegone, setting for Walk 22.

Start the walk at the CAR PARK above **Laorca** (❶): walk down the narrow street, following signs for walking ROUTES 56 AND 58. You pass a small shrine and reach the piazza in front of the CHURCH (**1min**). Turn right up a narrow street (signs for ROUTES 56 AND 58) which leads out of the village. Go to the left of a wide flight of steps and soon pass the CEMETERY (❷), which is built into the hillside, before keeping keep left again to walk below some cultivated terraces. Turn up a concrete path beside a pink house, continuing uphill with occasional glimpses of the rock towers above and with views down to Lecco. Beside house No. 16 (**11min**), you leave the concrete path and turn left along a grassy little path signposted 'MADALE S MARTINO'. Climb a few steps to continue along, until you meet a concrete road (**15min**). (Written on the wall opposite is 'S MARTINO', with an arrow pointing left). Follow this road downhill. After eight minutes, at a left-hand bend, you will see a clear sign pointing right to S MARTINO (❸). Take this path, which has a high wire fence on the left (rock slide protection) and woodland to the right.

After a few minutes you will see a

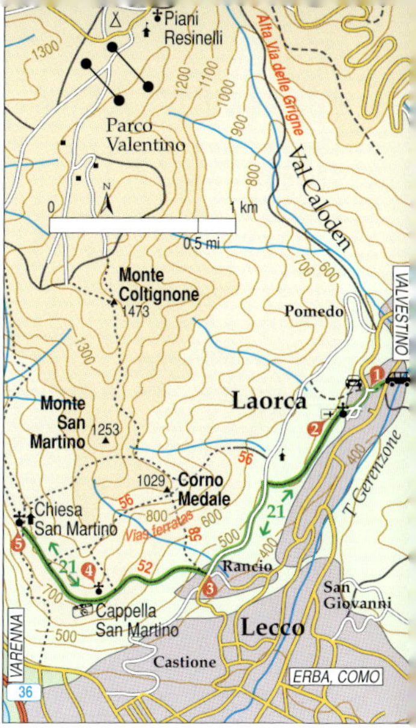

Left: the Cappella San Martino (top) and view from the door of the chapel across Lecco to Lago di Garlate

gap in the fence, where ROUTE 52 joins our path. You soon pass (and ignore!) a junction where a right turn leads to a *via ferrata.* At a large blue sign, aptly inscribed 'AVE MARIA', the climb starts in earnest. Follow the waymarks up the steep, stepped path, to eventually reach the small chapel of **San Martino** (**4**; **59min**). There is a balcony in front of this small building with a couple of welcoming benches. Far below is the sprawling mass of Lecco and, flowing from the end of Lake Como, the river Adda. The small lakes, Lago di Annone and Lago di Garlate, are also visible.

You can return from here the way you came but, for a good view northwards along Lake Como, continue on the path to the left of the chapel, passing a picnic table. After about nine minutes you come to a junction. Keep left to descend to the **Rifugio Riccardo Pizza** and, just beside it, the interesting **Chiesa San Martino** (**5**; **1h16min**), which was once a nunnery.

Return by retracing your steps to **Laorca** (**2h24min**).

Walk 22: PIANI D'ERNA

Distance/time: 6km/3.7mi; 1h44min

Grade: easy; mainly on good paths; a descent of 900m/2950ft

Equipment: see page 26. Walking poles. Refreshments are available at the Piani d'Erna and, in season, the Rifugio Stoppani.

Transport: to the Piani d'Erna. Follow Car tour 4 into Lecco. Turn left by the Erg garage as for the tour and then, where the tour turns right for Como, turn *left*, following signs for 'Funivia d'Erna'. Keep up this winding road until you reach the large car park at the lower cable car station (45° 51.791'N, 9° 25.680'E). Or, if you are driving directly from Bellagio, cross the *second* bridge over the river Adda into Lecco, following signs for Valsassina. Keep right at the first roundabout and then straight on, to go under the railway bridge. At an oddly shaped junction follow Valsassina again, going left and then right. Go through a set of traffic lights and at the roundabout 500m further on, follow signs for the *funivia*. from Lecco to the Funivia d'Erna; see 'Transport information' inside the back cover.

Nearest accommodation: Lecco, Bellagio or Varenna

Short walk: Sentiero Natura. 3.4km/2.1mi; 1h. Easy ups and downs of 150m/490ft overall; equipment/access as above. From the top cable car station walk down the track to the left, to the signposted 'INZIO SENTIERO NATURA'. This nature trail is well waymarked with red symbols, a circle on top of a line. It meanders around **Piani d'Erna** with many points of interest and some fine views of Resegone, Grigna Meridionale and down to Lecco (Picnic 10b). Good diagrams supplement the Italian text on the 20 information boards.

Resegone is a mountain of contrasts. The *funivia* rises up almost sheer cliffs but, when the top station is reached, alpine meadows greet you. This is a wonderful area, with a plethora of flowers in summer. With the coming of snow, it is transformed into a winter sports arena. A walk around Piani d'Erna is easy and most enjoyable, while the rocky towers and pointed peaks above challenge mountaineers and climbers. The Short and main walks combine well for a full day's outing.

The walk begins at the TOP CABLE CAR STATION (1) at **Piani d'Erna**: keep right at the first junction, to walk up to the **Croce Pizzo d'Erna** (2; **8min**; Picnic 10a). This airy vantage point gives a birds-eye view of Lecco far below, and across to the Resegone cliffs, under which our route descends. Notice the top of the *via ferrata*, a route only for the experienced and suitably equipped. Return to the

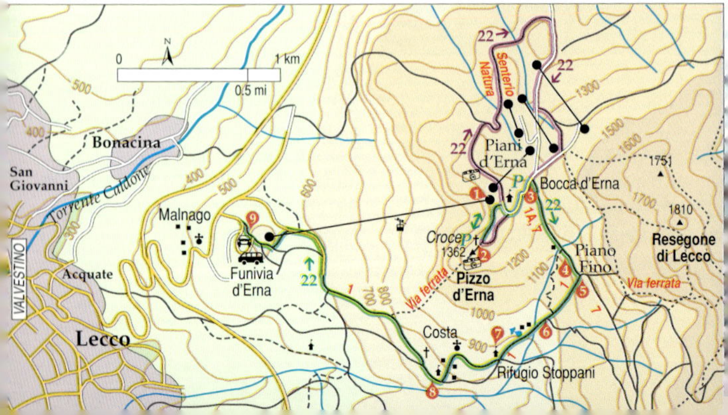

Hay stacks at Costa

junction outside the cable car station and turn right, passing the start of the nature trail and a bar/restaurant, to join a motorable track. Follow this down to the **Bocca d'Erna**, a wide grassy col (3; **19min**).

There are plenty of signposts here. Turn right along the first path, following the 1A and 7 routes to RIFUGIO STOPPANI. The path descends through woodland, after 11 minutes coming to a JUNCTION (4) beside a stream and an old building. Two paths here are signposted to RIFUGIO STOPPANI; take the left-hand path (the right-hand short-cut is narrow, rough and steep). You pass an old building with an adjoining open-sided barn and, in another two minutes reach a junction at **Piano Fino** (5; **38min**). Here we leave route 7 and follow ROUTE 1.

Bear right downhill. In about 13 minutes you come to the junction where the 'short-cut' rejoins the main path; above are the steep cliffs below Piani d'Erna. Three minutes later, at another JUNCTION (6), continue on ROUTE 1, going right and quickly crossing a small stream. A little further on, you pass some houses from where there is an excellent view back to the craggy summit of Resegone. Carry on to a SPRING, complete with ladle, in a little old building, and enjoy a drink of crystal-clear water before reaching **Rifugio Stoppani** (7; **1h04min**).

Below the *rifugio* turn right and descend again. Just above the attractive group of houses called Costa, *do* leave the path to see the small glass-fronted CHAPEL on the right — a poignant reminder of the dangers of hill walking and mountaineering. Inside are plaques dedicated to local climbers who have died on mountains all around the world — the first was recorded in 1887 and some were as young as fourteen.

Costa (8; **1h15min**) is set in a delightful position, surrounded by green pastures where donkeys graze and hay is still gathered into traditional haystacks. Follow the waymarks through the houses and then turn right below the buildings, to pass a SHRINE. After about 12 minutes note a path heading off to the right — the start of the *via ferrata* that you saw at the Erna summit. Continue down the wide, easy path to an asphalt road, where you go straight ahead. Follow this road under the cables of the *funivia,* where you turn left on a path that leads back to the car park, bus stop and LOWER CABLE CAR STATION (9; **1h44min**).

Walk 23: IN THE TRIANGULO LARIANO

Distance/time: 7.5km/4.7mi; 2h30min
Grade: ● easy; an undulating ridge walk on grassy paths, with under 400m/1300ft of ascent/descent overall
Equipment: see page 26. Refreshments are available at Colma.
Transport: 🚗 From Bellagio drive south towards Asso. About 1.5km before Asso, turn right up through Sormano, following Car tour 4 as far as Colma, where there is parking on either side of the ridge (45° 52.969'N, 9° 13.735'E).
Nearest accommodation: Bellagio
Short walk: Monte Croce. 4.3km/2.6mi; 1h23min. ● easy, with just 180m/590ft of ascent/descent. Equipment and access as main walk. Follow the main walk as far as **Monte Croce** (❻; 43min) for good views and return the same way.

This is an undemanding hike over rolling hills in the pastoral countryside of the Triangolo Lariano, the triangular-shaped area between the two arms of Lake Como. We follow a section of the long-distance footpath, the Dorsale del Triangolo Lariano, which links Brunate, above Como, to Bellagio. Starting high above the lake, we think you will love this out- and-back ridge walk, which is exhilarating and ideal for a short day.

This walk starts across the road from the OBSERVATORY at **Colma,** where you will find a path beside a MEMORIAL dedicated to cyclists and behind a log barrier. Follow this for a few metres into the field, and then strike off uphill, heading towards a fence. Go through the STILE ahead and carry on up the grassy ridge, passing a water hole, to reach the flat grassy TOP of **Monte Falo** (❷; **8min**; Picnic 12).

From here you can see your route ahead, stretching all the way to Monte Palanzone. Continue downhill to a COL (❸), which you cross to climb up the next slope. Pass through some patchy woodland, to reach the top of another grassy hillock, where you will see a clear RED AND YELLOW WAYMARK

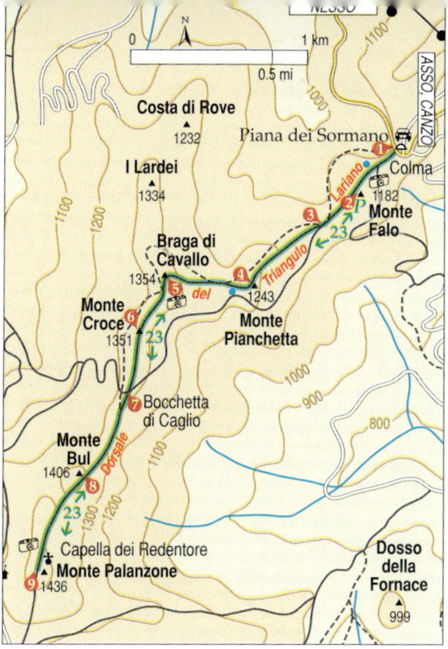

on a stone (**Monte Pianchetta**; 4; **23min**).

You are now on open ground, with trees only on the northern side and clear views to the south. Follow the path to the right of another water hole, to pass a waymark post and carry on along the ridge. A track joins from the right; where it heads off to the right again, go straight ahead, past a waymarked tree (and perhaps a sign as well). This rather rough path climbs steeply on the edge of the open ridge to the next TOP, **Braga di Cavallo** (5; **39min**).

Walk left along the ridge, on the fairly level path, now enjoying good views on both sides. The hill village of Veleso can be clearly seen and far below, to the right, is Lake Como. In another minute the same track you met earlier merges with your route again. Either follow this track (now little more than a wide grassy path) or climb the few extra metres to cross **Monte Croce** (6; **43min**) and walk down from there along the ridge. *(The Short walk returns from Monte Croce via the outgoing route.)*

Either route will take you to the grassy col of **Bocchetta di Caglio** (7; **49min**). Fork left here, away from the wide path and, following waymarks, climb the steep slope to the SUMMIT of **Monte Bul** (8). From here continue easily along the ridge (the large building on the western slopes is Rifugio Riella) to **Monte Palanzone** (9; **1h20min**). Here you will find the **Cappella dei Redentore**, a very unusual, obelisk-shaped chapel with a small cross on top. This is a beautiful, quiet spot to relax and enjoy the views, especially on a sunny day. Westwards and below, Torno sits on the shores of Lake Como, while in the opposite direction lies Sormano and the other villages above Asso. However, the most impressive outlook must be to the northwest, with the craggy mountain of Grigna (Walk 20) dominating the scene.

Return by retracing your steps to **Colma** (**2h30min**).

View to Monte San Primo from Colma (near Picnic 12)

Walk 24: PARCO MONTE SAN PRIMO

See also photograph page 95
Distance/time: 7.1km/4.4mi; 2h48min
Grade: ● moderate, but with a very steep and strenuous climb of 545m/1788ft to the summit of Monte San Primo. (To avoid this very steep ascent, you can gain the height more gradually by following the main walk in reverse. From the car park, turn left along a narrow asphalt road up to Alpe del Borgo. Take the rising path behind the upper building, heading slightly to the right (well to the right of a small ski lift). Once you are on the ridge, the way to Monte San Primo is easily followed. Return the same way from the summit.)
Equipment: see page 26. Walking poles. Refreshments are available near the car park and at the Rifugio Martina (open in season and on all fine weekends).
Transport: 🚗 From Bellagio (Car tour 4) follow signs for Lecco and then for Erba/Lecco. Keep straight on along the road to Guello. After about 4.5km turn right for 'Piano Rancio' and 'Monte Primo'. Just before Piano Rancio turn right to reach the Parco Monte San Primo, where you turn left to park in the large car park opposite and above the restaurant La Baita (45° 55.404'N, 9° 13.833'E).
Nearest accommodation: Bellagio
***Short walk:* Rifugio Martina.** 3.5km/2.2mi; 1h04min. ● Easy, with an ascent/descent of about 100m/330ft. Trainers will suffice. Access as above. Follow the main walk as far as the Rifugio Martina (❸; 34min), for great views and to enjoy refreshments on the terrace. Return the same way.

Monte San Primo is the backdrop to Bellagio, the lakeside town that sits so picturesquely on the tip of the Triangolo Lariano (see Walk 23). The inverted Y-shape of Lake Como was created by the Adda Glacier, which, millions of years ago, split at this point to carve out the arms that lead down to Lecco and Como. This unusual shape is best seen from the summit of Monte San Primo — a viewpoint that affords one of the best and most extensive views over what many people believe to be the loveliest of the Italian Lakes.

The walk begins at the CAR PARK in **Parco Monte San Primo** (❶): walk back down the road and turn left by a large building where a signpost indicates ROUTE 1 (the Dorsale del Triangolo Lariano walk, described in Walk 23). Go between some old houses to reach the end of the asphalt road and enter woodland, soon crossing a stream. Continue along the gravel road for nine minutes, then pass a large building and go through gates.

In another six minutes you enter the grassy **Alpe delle Ville** (❷). Here we *leave* route No. 1, which goes right to Bellagio. A few metres further along the track, keep left towards 'RIFUGIO MARTINA' and 'MONTE S PRIMO' (ROUTE 39). You pass through more gates. Follow the track across open ground and walk up towards ALPE DEL PICET. Beyond another gate, climb steps to reach **Alpe del Picet** and the **Rifugio Martina** (❸; **34min**). From here you have a magnificent view over Lake Como. *(The Short walk returns from here.)*

Climb a few more steps and then take a signposted path to the left. Beside the uppermost building,

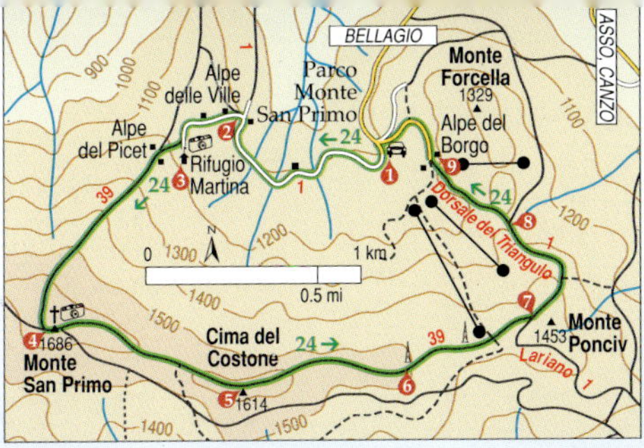

and a huge boulder, turn right alongside a wire fence to continue up the narrow path into scrubby trees. The ascent becomes ever steeper as you now clamber along the crest of a ridge, at first through beech woods and then through scrubby trees once more.

Finally you emerge on the summit ridge and turn left, to quickly reach the TOP of **Monte San Primo** (❹; **1h35min**). The inscription on the cross reads 'Justice, Freedom, Peace — give your name to these'. The effort has all been worthwhile — the 360-degree panorama, on a clear day, is stunning. You will be able to pick out mountains you may have climbed and many more you would like to! Starting in the south, look across Monte Palanzone and beyond, to the Lombardy Plain. Westwards is Monte Rosa, dominating the long skyline of Alps above the nearby peaks of Monte di Tremezzo and Monte Generoso. To the north, over Bellagio on the tip of the Triangolo Lariano, is the upper stretch of Lake Como, the foreground to more Alps. Finally, in the east is the Grigna massif and the mountains above Lecco.

From the summit, walk easily along the crest in an easterly direction, over the top of **Cima del Costone** (❺), ignoring a wide grassy path on the right. Continue past a little hut and an ugly telecom MAST (❻). From here drop down past another MAST and the top of a ski lift, to reach a wide, grassy COL and a signpost (❼; **2h17min**). Here you meet ROUTE 1 again, which you follow under the northern side of **Monte Ponciv**, to meet the crest of another ridge. Follow this downhill, with more wonderful views, to a signposted COL (❽; **2h32min**) where you turn left (still ROUTE 1).

Descend through attractive woods for a short way, before emerging once more on open ground, from where you can survey the day's route. It is a very colourful scene, especially late in the year, when the beech trees turn to gold and are bathed in warm autumn sunlight. Follow the path down to the **Alpe del Borgo** (❾; **2h42min**) and, from the far side of the farm buildings, take the narrow asphalt road back to the CAR PARK (❶; **2h48min**).

View north across Lake Como from Monte San Primo

Walk 25: AROUND MONTE BRIONE

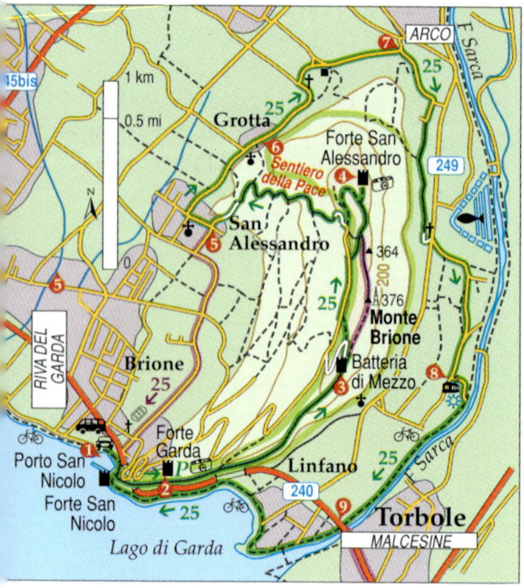

Transport: Drive along the lakefront from either Riva del Garda or Torbole (Car tour 5) and park in the large car park at Porto San Nicolo (45° 52.696'N, 10° 51.437'E). to Porto San Nicolo; see 'Transport informtion' inside the back cover. Alight at the Hotel Brione, then walk towards Torbole to reach the large car park. Or, for an easy and very pleasant alternative, simply walk from either resort to Porto San Nicolo by following the lakeside paths.

Nearest accommodation: Torbole or Riva del Garda

Distance/time: 11.2km/6.9mi; 3h04min

Grade: ● easy; mainly on clear paths and quiet country roads; 200m/650ft of ascents/descents

Equipment: see page 26. Refreshments available in San Alessandro

Short walk: Forte San Alessandro. 5km/3mi; 1h49min. ● Grade, equipment and access as above. Follow the main walk to the 59min-point at 4 and return the same way.

The wedge-shaped rocky outcrop of Monte Brione at the head of Lake Garda, which separates Riva del Garda from Torbole, cannot be missed. Left behind by the glacier that carved out the lake, this hill offers excellent views along Lake Garda and, to the north, up the Sarca Valley. Monte Brione's strategic position is such that it has several ruined forts, tunnels and bunkers along its length, but today all is peaceful. This walk along the ridge is full of interest, while the return, through the quiet agricultural valley, is in stark contrast to the busy coastal resorts.

Monte Brione from the eastern shore of Lake Garda (Picnic 13)

Start out at the CAR PARK (1) at **Porto San Nicolo**: walk along the CYCLE TRACK towards the road tunnel and, just before it, turn right. To the left and above the large building of **Forte San Nicolo**, take a flight of steps that leads up to a hairpin bend on a road. Here you will find an information board and map beside a path, signposted SENTIERO DELLA PACE — 'Path of Peace' (**5min**). Walk up the stepped path, quickly reaching a viewpoint overlooking Lake Garda. You now follow the cliff edge closely, coming to fine viewpoints (Picnic 13) across to Torbole, once a little fishing village with a picturesque harbour, now a bustling resort favoured by sports enthusiasts. There is also an extensive view down the lake, busy with the bright sails of boats and windsurfers. The large concreted area is the remains of **Forte Garda** (2; **12min**).

Higher up, you walk beside olive trees on your left and look down over Riva del Garda, with its grand castle, and across to the spiny ridges of Rocchetta (Walk 37). Below, to your right, are the vineyards and orchards beside the river Sarca, through which the walk returns. Squeeze through a heavy-duty stile (3; **41min**), to reach the imposing **Batteria di Mezzo**, a grisly reminder of wartime conflict.

The path now leaves the ridge, going through another squeeze-stile on the far side of the fort and descending by a gravel road through an avenue of Lombardy pines. (You *could* continue up to the summit of **Monte Brione**, but it bristles with television masts and only has limited views through the trees). At the first bend, carry straight on along a path through woodland. When you meet an asphalt road, turn right, and then turn right again on a gravel track at the first fork, to regain the ridge. Continue on to the extensive remains of **Forte San Alessandro** (4; **59min**) and follow the path through the ruins to a fine viewpoint. Here you look out to Arco with its fairytale castle, and across vineyards extending northwards up the Sarca Valley.

Retrace your steps from the fort for less than two minutes, to take a path on your right (clear and well-used, but with *no waymarks*). This doubles back through massive fortifications. The path drops down to a small grassy area, where you continue around to the right, soon ignoring another path off to the right. Go through some tall, old METAL GATES to reach the end of the asphalt road (**1h09min**). Here turn right down a gravel road, passing through more METAL GATES. There are further wartime remains as you descend the ever-narrowing track, which at one point becomes little more than a path. Twist downhill, eventually leaving the trees and coming into olive terraces, some newly planted. Join a cobbled and concreted road and follow this until, as you pass a rather grand house entrance, the road becomes asphalt. Just before coming to a junction on the outskirts of **San Alessandro** (5; **1h31min**), you will see the grand old VILLA LUTTI on your right. (If you wish to shorten your day and return direct to the start of the walk, you could carry straight on here to the main road. Turn left and follow the wide pavement straight back to Porto San Nicolo.)

Turn right, now with an even better view of the villa, to meet a crossroads by a CHURCH, where you turn right again. You leave San Alessandro behind and walk along the road, ignoring a left turn opposite a chapel. Carry

Vineyards in the Sarca Valley

straight on through **Grotta** (❻; **1h40min**), where the sheer cliffs of Monte Brione loom menacingly over the small village. Beyond, you continue past fields of corn and vineyards, as the road bears away from the cliffs. At a junction, turn right beside a SHRINE. Keep to the right at the next junction and enjoy the colourful vineyards in this fertile area. Looking up the **Sarca Valley**, Arco castle can be seen, but the many pylons associated with the nearby generating station mar the view. After nine minutes, beside a large old building (**1h58min**), turn right, rounding the northern edge of Monte Brione.

In another five minutes, just before reaching the main road, turn right on a road with a CLOSED TO TRAFFIC SIGN (❼). Where the road bends right towards some houses, keep straight on along a track between vines, orchards and vegetable plots on what was the old road. This climbs slightly, soon becoming a path through olive terraces. You walk above a house, then the path widens out into a track again, eventually meeting the driveway to the house. Follow this for a few metres, to join the main road beside a wooden CRUCIFIX (**2h13min**).

Go straight across and follow the surfaced road opposite through fields of fruit and corn. Some 600 metres along, at a Y-fork, keep right. Then, just before a HYDRO-ELECTRIC STATION, turn left on a CYCLE TRACK (❽), passing a metal barrier. Follow it to the right behind a WATER TREATMENT PLANT. This cycle route follows the top of a flood protection dyke and is well used — keep to one side and listen out for cyclists. The **river Sarca**, which feeds Lake Garda, is below to your left and the road is lined with beautiful flowering shrubs.

When you come to the main road on the outskirts of **Torbole** (❾; **2h39min**), turn left to reach the centre. To return to Porto San Nicolo and Riva del Garda, cross the road and follow the CYCLE ROUTE again, to reach the lakeside. Continue on the cycle/walkway, past windsurfing schools and camping sites, beneath Monte Brione. You round the end of the cliffs by the road tunnel, to pass Forte San Nicolo, beyond which is the CAR PARK AND BUS STOP at **Porto San Nicolo** (❶; **3h04min**).

Walk 26: FROM ARCO TO COLODRI AND MONTE COLT

Distance/time: 8km/5mi; 3h25min
Grade: ● ⁂ moderate, with some 500m/1640ft of ascent/descent. All paths are steep, but the initial climb to Colodri is not difficult. Beyond there you must be sure-footed and have a head for heights: very steep, exposed paths, rough in places, slippery when wet. All paths CAI waymarked 431/431b
Equipment: see page 26. Walking poles. Refreshments are available at Arco.
Transport: 🚗 to/from Arco (well signposted from Riva del Garda and Torbole; detour on Car tour 5); ample parking near the town centre (45° 559.097'N, 10° 53.242'E). 🚌 to/from Arco; see 'Transport information' inside the back cover. Alight at the bus station and walk down Viale Roma past the Evangelical Church, with its multi-coloured roof, to Via Marconi opposite the tourist office. Turn right and cross the road into a small park with an old yew tree in the centre. The walk starts at the church on the far side of this park.
Nearest accommodation: Torbole or Riva del Garda

Short Walk: Croce di Colodri. 3.7km/2.3mi; 1h34min. ● Easy; equipment/access as above; ascent/descent of 200m. Follow the main walk to **Colodri** (❸; 54min), then retrace your steps to Santa Maria di Laghel. Now pick up the main walk again at the 3h05min-point to return to Arco.

From the fertile Sarca Valley the ruins of Arco Castle, perched on a rocky tower, are quite a landmark. On this walk we take you through the fascinating old town of Arco, up past the castle gates and beyond, along a craggy limestone ridge. You are assured of fine views, but you may also see skilled rock climbers and possibly daredevils base-jumping (parachuting) from the high cliffs.

Start the walk at the front of the parish church of **Santa Maria Assunta** in **Arco** (❶), with its wonderfully carved wooden doors. Cross the Piazza III Novembre. Keep to the left of this square and go up a short street, only a few metres long, then turn left on VIA DEL DOSSO (sign: CASTELLO,PARCO). Climb gently through the attractive old town, where the windows and balconies are decorated with flowers. Turn right up VICOLO SCALE (just before Via Stranfora) and then go right again immediately, up what looks like a short cul-de-sac. Take steps here that lead up in lazy zigzags through terraces of olive trees, giving lovely views over the town's rooftops. Ignore a path down to the right. When you meet the drive to the **Castello di Arco** (**15min**), turn left. (Or first turn right to visit the castle; although ruined, it has some fine 14th-century frescoes and is an excellent viewpoint.)

After turning left you quickly pass a path off left beside a picnic table. Below you can see the remains of the old town wall as you head towards an asphalt road. Turn right along this road, to walk beneath sheer limestone cliffs and above a shallow valley full of olive trees. Join a cobbled road which leads past the higher Stations of the Cross to **Santa Maria di Laghel** (❷; **29min**).

Just before this little church, and on your right, is a signposted path (MONTE COLT, CENIGA), the **Sentiero dei Lecci**. Follow this past THREE CRUCIFIXES and up into the trees. Along the way there are several information boards in English and good waymarks, which you need to *follow closely* as you near the SUMMIT of **Colodri** (❸; **54min**). An old METAL CROSS stands on this rocky outcrop, from where there is a fine view down over Arco Castle and across the fertile plain at the head of Lake Garda.

Retrace your steps for about two minutes/100m, to a waymarked path going right (COLODRI, COLT, CENIGA). Follow this path around a rocky hollow, above which you can see the waymarks. The going is now quite rough, over serrated limestone boulders. In a few minutes you come to the edge of a steep cliff. From this dramatic viewpoint you can see your route along the ridge and up the vine-filled Sarca Valley towards Dro. Turn left along the cliff and then drop steeply for a few metres, where *care is needed.* An easier path then leads you back to the cliff edge beside a PYLON (**1h14min**). Look back and to the right to appreciate the vertical limestone cliffs on which you were just standing.

Continue following the waymarks, turning right at a T-junction, to quickly come to some terraces where you meet a track and a signpost. Turn right for MONTE COLT, passing a small farm and walking beside a drystone wall. You enter the trees again and

follow the narrow path to another fine viewpoint over the valley. Carry on to reach a JUNCTION (❹; **1h41min**). (You could cut the walk short here by turning left, following the sign for Laghel, along the path that zigzags easily down to rejoin the main route at the 2h44min-point).

Turn right and, one minute later, fork left for CENIGA and MONTE COLT. The path twists through the woods, limestone outcrops and serrated limestone rocks, passing the unnoticed tops of **Monte Colt** and **Prea**, the highest points, but covered with trees. Towards the end of the ridge the trees become more scrubby and the limestone rock much more prominent. Descend to eventually reach **Croce di Colt** (❺; **2h01min**), marked by an old CROSS which has seen better days. From here there is a fine view over the Sarca Valley.

Walk back a few metres from the cross, where you will see a sign (CENIGA). Turn right and, keeping a keen eye out for the waymarks, traverse an area of sloping limestone. Beyond the limestone the waymarks are more easily seen as they guide you through trees and then down the steep, scree-strewn hillside, sometimes along narrow ledges, sometimes in tight zigzags. *Go carefully here; it is dangerous when wet — and ignore* any blue waymarks you may spot, as these seem to indicate an even more 'sporting' and direct descent! You eventually reach a path on the floor of a narrow valley, beside a PYLON (**2h25min**).

Turn left uphill. You meet and keep to the left of a wire fence and, at the top of your climb, pass by a house. Just beyond, you join a concrete driveway and the path that has descended from the ridge of Monte Colt (**2h44min**).

Carry straight on to an asphalt road, where you keep ahead. Continue downhill into the fertile valley, passing small farms, to return to the church at **Laghel** (**3h05min**). From here follow the STATIONS OF THE CROSS (depicted in relief and quite beautiful) down the cobbled road, enjoying a superb view of the castle through olive groves. Beyond a bar you reach the asphalt road again. Turn right downhill and, in about three minutes/200m, turn left to go under an old archway in the town walls and enter **Arco**. Keep right and downhill, along VIA STRANFORA, passing an open air washing area and water tap. This is a fascinating part of the old town, untainted by the trappings of tourism. Keep straight on and pass the church of San Bernardino, to rejoin your outward route in VIA DEL DOSSO. Then retrace your steps to **Santa Maria Assunta** (**3h25min**).

View north along the Monte Colt ridge and over the Sarca Valley

Walk 27: MONTE STIVO CIRCUIT

Distance/time: 9.8km/6mi; 3h43min

Grade: ● strenuous; mainly on good mountain paths and tracks, ascent/descent of 810m/2657ft. Partly waymarked Route 608.

Equipment: see page 26. Walking poles. Refreshments are available just below the summit from the Rifugio Monte Stivo P Marchetti.

Transport: 🚗 Drive from either Torbole or Riva del Garda (Car tour 5) and head for Arco, until you pick up signs for Rovereto. After crossing the river Sarca, turn right at the roundabout and then turn left for Bolognano/Monte Velo. Keep following brown signs for Monte Velo — a long climb on a narrow road. At Santa Barbara turn left beside the water trough (there's a parking sign at the left). Park 0.8km uphill, opposite a brown cabin called San Antonio's Bar (the name is on its far side; 45° 54.022'N, 10° 56.615'E). Allow 40 minutes' driving.

Nearest accommodation: Riva del Garda or Torbole

Short walk: Castello del Castil and Le Prese. 4.2km/2.6mi; about 1h30min. ● Moderate; ascent/descent 300m/985ft; equipment/access as above. Follow the main walk to ❸ (53min). We suggest that you go a little way up the grassy ridge of Le Prese or, more easily, up the track for some fine views. To return, follow the main walk from the 3h14min-point.

A lovely drive is just a bonus at the start of a superb walk. This high and beautiful mountain, with its open grassy slopes, is away from the tourist resorts and well within the capabilities of any fit walker. On a clear day the broad summit of Monte Stivo is a perfect setting to appreciate the wonderful panoramic views.

Start out at SAN ANTONIO'S BAR above **Santa Barbara** (❶): go along the asphalt road past a SHRINE and a MANEGE, then turn left at the BAITA CASTIL building, to walk through cultivated fields. To your right you can see Le Prese, the ridge you will soon climb. Where the asphalt ends at a three-way junction, go straight on along a two-wheel track. After about 12 minutes you reach the end of the track near a small building on the right. Keep left beside a hedge and cross an old terrace, to take a narrow path that quickly enters woodland. In less than three minutes you come to a signposted junction (**15min**). To find the castle, walk down to the water trough and seek out a narrow path behind it. Climb this to reach the ruins of **Castello del Castil** (❷; **19min**) — in a wonderful position, commanding fine views over Arco and the surrounding mountains.

Return to the signposted junction and turn left towards PRESE and STIVO on ROUTE 608. This narrow path climbs through woodland, sometimes quite steeply. Eventually you emerge on a broad ridge and meet a track beside a BENCH and SHRINE by a sign, '**Le Prese**' (❸; **53min**). From here you can see the *rifugio* just below the summit — looking much closer than it is! The little path that goes up Le Prese's wide grassy ridge is your next target.

Turn left up the track and, after only a few metres, take a short-cut path that soon meets the track again. Cross straight over and begin to climb up the steep ridge. It is hard work, but the views are ever-improving. Higher up, follow the edge of a cliff; after about 45 minutes of strenuous climbing you

The steep cliffs of Monte Stivo, from Le Prese

reach a rocky outcrop at the TOP OF THE RIDGE (**1h38min**). The steep cliffs that fall from the summit of Monte Stivo can be clearly seen.

Descend a short way from here through dwarf pine and reach the cliff edge again, beside a rickety old fence. Joining a clear path, follow the cliff top, still climbing, until the path leaves it to cross the open hillside towards the *rifugio*.

A few metres before the **Rifugio Monte Stivo P Marchetti** (❹; **2h11min**), you meet the main waymarked path, which is your route of descent. The *rifugio* has a fine outlook, but with the summit and its promised panoramic views only a few minutes walk away, you may want to reach the top first. Turn right at the building and go up the waymarked path to the SUMMIT of **Monte Stivo** (❺; **2h17min**). There is a large CROSS here, with a metal box holding a visitors' book. The views will take your breath away, and a viewpoint indicator will help put names to the many peaks visible. Clearly seen are the mountains of the Brenta, Presenello, Adamello and Popiccole Dolomiti Groups. The summit area is broad and grassy, a fine place to relax.

To return, retrace your steps to the *rifugio* (excellent refreshments). Then turn left, following the waymarks and passing your ascent route. Below on open slopes are the farm buildings of Malga Stivo — your next objective. Follow the easy graded path in long zigzags down the hillside, taking a steeper short-cut if you wish, to reach **Malga Stivo** (❻; **2h46min**). (Or bypass the buildings by descending the grassy slopes to reach the track by the bottom of the goods hoist that supplies the *rifugio*).

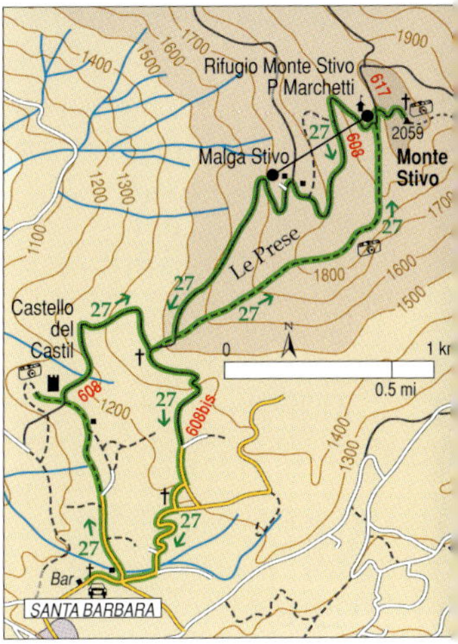

From the buildings, follow a track easily down to the LE PRESE SIGN you first met at the 53min-point (❸; **3h14min**). Continue down the track to drop more steeply through woodland, and keep right where another track turns off left. Asphalt comes under foot and, very quickly, you fork right to carry on gently downhill beside open fields. Pass a CROSS and then a house; then, at a junction, turn right. Follow this road back to the SAN ANTONIO'S BAR (❶) above **Santa Barbara** (**3h43min**).

Walk 28: CIMA DELLE POZZETTE (MONTE BALDO)

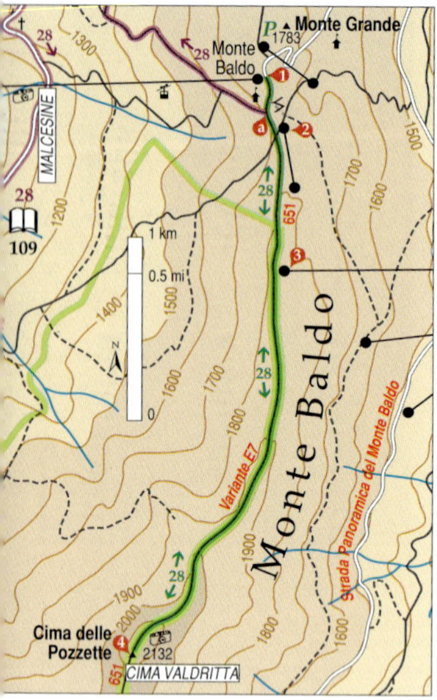

Transport: , or to the *funivia* at Malcesine, then to Monte Baldo station. Drive some 14km south from Torbole (Car tour 5). In Malcesine turn left at the first traffic lights to the car park for the *funivia* (45° 45.986'N, 10° 48.773'E). from Riva del Garda, Torbole or Limone. From the ferry terminal turn left alongside the harbour and then right by Hotel San Marco, to reach the square in front of the municipal buildings. Walk up the road to the left of these, to the main road through the town (the bus station is opposite). Turn left along this road and then turn right at the traffic lights, following signs for the *funivia*. Allow 10 minutes. : see 'Transport information' inside the back cover. From the bus station walk back towards Riva del Garda and then turn right at the first traffic lights, following signs for the *funivia*.

Nearest accommodation: Malcesine, Riva del Garda, Torbole or Limone sul Garda

Alternative walk: From the Monte Baldo cable car station down to Malcesine. See page 108.

Distance/time: 7km/4.3mi; 2h40min

Grade: ● easy-moderate, on well waymarked, but sometimes rough paths (Route 651), with an ascent/descent of 400m/1350ft

Equipment: see page 26. Walking poles. Refreshments are available at Monte Baldo cable car station.

Monte Baldo is the long high ridge which dominates the skyline above Malcesine. Often referred to as the 'Botanical Garden of Europe', and with two nature reserves, the slopes of this giant mountain are host to a wide variety of flora, including some unique to this area. The top of the ridge, however, is windswept, with sparse vegetation, and is susceptible to rapid changes in weather conditions. Be prepared for a drop in temperature, as thunderstorms can strike quickly, and low clouds form thick mist without warning. There are many waymarked paths, but the two walks we describe (main and Alternative) involve no steep climbs and can readily be combined to provide a full and varied day in the hills.

The walk begins at the **Monte Baldo** CABLE CAR STATION (❶) above Malcesine. Turn right downhill, past two bars. A few metres past an ELECTRICITY SUBSTATION, at a junction, keep ahead towards a small SKI LIFT (❷). *(But for the Alternative walk, descend to the right here.)* Keep to the right of the ski lift, following ROUTE 651 up

The Monte Baldo cable car rising from Malcesine

through rocky terrain. Higher up, the well-waymarked path crosses easier ground, to reach the top of a CHAIR LIFT (3; **28min**).

At this point you can clearly see your objective, Cima del Pozzette, further along the ridge. You quickly go through a wooden fence and enter a nature reserve. Then the well-trodden path climbs gently across grassy areas interspersed with dwarf pine. Further on the path becomes more rocky and a little rougher, but the views continually improve until you gain the undistinguished and unmarked SUMMIT of **Cima del Pozzette** (4; **1h30min**). The views over the southern end of Lake Garda are amazing, but the mountains draw the eye. The whole northern horizon is a long chain of snow-capped peaks and, if you are lucky enough to have a very clear day, you can see Monte Rosa far to the west. Far away to the east are the Julian Alps of Slovenia.

(The path, route 651, carries on along the ridge, bypassing the next summit, Cima del Longino, to reach the highest peak on the Baldo range, Cima Valdritta. While this continuation is clearly waymarked, the going on Monte Baldo is much more difficult south of Cima del Pozzette; we would only recommend it for experienced mountain walkers prepared for a full day's outing.)

The return walk, as you retrace your steps, is even more rewarding. The distant views can be fully appreciated as you descend easily back to the **Monte Baldo** CABLE CAR STATION (1; **2h40min**). Be prepared to queue here when you arrive late in the day — or if the weather closes in!

View north from Cima delle Pozzette along the Monte Baldo ridge to Monte Altissimo di Nago (similar to the views from Picnic 14)

Alternative walk: From the Monte Baldo cable car station down to Malcesine. 8km/5mi; 2h30min. **See map opposite.** ● Easy but steep descent of 1650m/5400ft, *hard on the knees*. Equipment/access as main walk. Refreshments also available in season at Rifugio Prai and near San Michele station.

Start out by following the main walk towards ❷ but, just before the SKI LIFT turn right on a path signposted to PRAI, SAN MICHELE FUNIVIA (ⓐ). This rough path, ROUTE 11, descends steeply over open ground below the cables of the *funivia,* with fine views down to Lake Garda and the mountains beyond.

After 35min you pass two benches beside an excellent VIEWPOINT (ⓑ) overlooking Malcesine. Turn right, still on ROUTE 11, following a sign for PRAI. Now traverse fenced alpine grazing, stepping from field to field through squeeze stiles. After about six minutes the path turns sharp left above a building, which has a V-shaped concrete wall — a defence against avalanches. Head down to the **Rifugio Prai** (ⓒ; 46min).

On the far side of the hut, join a concrete track that leads down to a road, suitable only for 4-wheel drive vehicles, and turn left following signs for the FUNIVIA and IL SIGNOR. After about seven minutes ignore a rough track joining from the right and, three minutes later, reach another good viewpoint. You now drop more steeply, the trees become thicker, and you soon pass under the cables again. (This is a good spot for photography, as you can get both the upward and downward cars.) Continue on to a SHRINE, **Il Signor**, which forms a covered way across your route (ⓓ; **1h16min**).

After a further 12 minutes take a wide path to the right (a short-cut), and soon turn left at a junction. Rejoin the road, under the cables once more, and turn right. Just four minutes later, look for a path on the left, signposted to S MICHELE. Follow this to a junction and turn right to reach the middle *funivia* station, **San Michele** (ⓔ;**1h52min**).

From the car park in front of the station follow the road to the right and then left downhill, to walk back towards the cables. Just before you reach them, turn right down a concrete lane from where there are fine views down to Malcesine and join a cobbled path (which can be very slippery when wet).

After about four minutes take a path that forks left ('PAIER' may be painted faintly in red on a rock). This path, covered in slippery gravel, soon passes under the cables and then widens out and runs past olive groves, with great views down through the scrubby trees. You come to an asphalt road, the VIA PANORAMICA, by a SHRINE (❺; **2h05min**).

Turn left and, after about 100m, turn sharp right down a narrow road (VIA PAIER). Only two minutes later, leave this road by going right on a surfaced path (a 'long-cut'). You quickly rejoin the road and turn right to come to an arched SHRINE where the road ends, at **Paier** (❹; **2h11min**).

Pass under the arch and, almost immediately, fork right on a cobbled path, which zigzags down steeply. Look out for a bench with a superb view over Malcesine. Pass a path coming in from the right and continue, now less steeply, through olive groves. You meet a concrete road and, at the bottom, bear right downhill by a little SHRINE on your right, quickly returning to the CAR PARK for the CABLE CAR STATION in **Malcesine** (❼; **2h30min**).

Walk 29: MADONNA DELL'ACCOGLIENZA CIRCUIT

Distance/time: 7km/4.3mi; 1h57min
Grade: ● easy; on quiet roads, good tracks and paths; ascent/descent of about 275m/900ft
Equipment: see page 26. Walking shoes will suffice. Refreshments are available at Malcesine.
Transport: 🚗, ⛴ or 🚌 to Malcesine. Park behind the ferry terminal (45° 45.849'N, 10° 48.508'E). If you arrive by bus, from the station walk along the main road towards Verona, to join the main walk at the 4min-point (the bottom of the Via Panoramica).

Nearest accommodation: Malcesine, Riva del Garda, Torbole or Limone sul Garda
***Shorter Madonna dell'Accoglienza crcuit*:** 4.3km/2.6mi; 1h22min. ● Grade, equipment, access as above. Follow the main walk to the 58min-point at **Paier** (❹), then follow *Alternative* walk 28 (opposite) from the 2h11min-point back to the lower *funivia* station in **Malcesine** (❼). From there follow the walk from the 1h52min-point at (❼) to walk back to the bus station or ferry terminal (❶).

Malcesine is a delightful old town clustered around a tiny harbour, with a magnificent Scaligeri castle perched on a little promontory. Within its walls is the fascinating Museum of the Lake (Museo del Lago), which houses many historical exhibits. On this short walk we take you up the hillside behind Malcesine, through olive orchards, to a secluded spot where a graceful Madonna looks out over the scenic beauty of the town, Lake Garda and the mountains beyond.

Begin the walk at the FERRY TERMINAL AND PORT (❶) in **Malcesine**. From Piazza Porto, turn right and then take the first fork to the left. This leads to a wide road, with toilets on the left. Cross the road and climb the stepped, cobbled path on the right (VIA PISORT) to come to the main road (**4min**).

Turn right here and, after a few metres, cross the road to find the start of VIA PANORAMICA. Follow this uphill but, in under 50m, turn left uphill on VIA CREVE, a concrete road with red/white waymarks. Now walk between olive terraces (olives are an important source of revenue in this region). After five minutes you reach a superb viewpoint looking back over Malcesine and its castle. Just beyond the viewpoint, cross a rough road and carry on up narrow Via Creve (between houses Nos. 11 and 13). This soon

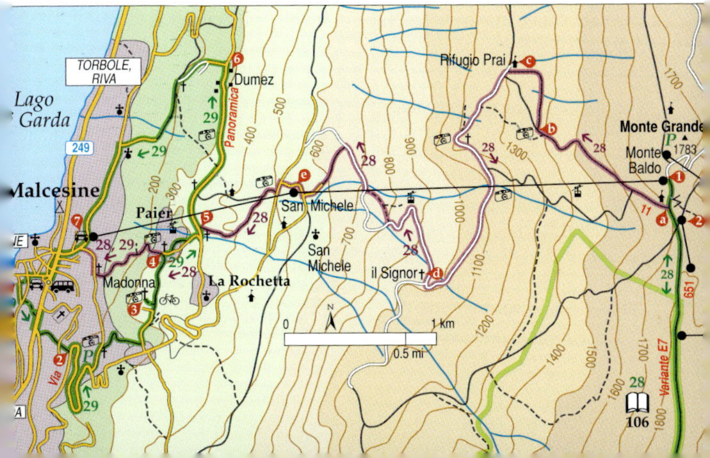

The Scaligeri castles

For 127 years, from the middle of the 13th century, the Scaligeri family ruled Verona — ruthlessly taking the city, but later establishing peace. From this centre they spread their influence around Lake Garda, building several defensive castles, the best known being those at Sirmione and Malcesine. They also extended and used others, such as those at Arco and the Rocca at Riva del Garda. Arco Castle is now ruined, and the Rocca has been altered over the years, but the moated castle at Sirmione and the one at Malcesine, perched on a promontory and standing guard over the town, retain a fairytale appearance with distinctive fishtail-shaped battlements.

Photograph: Scaligeri castle at Malcesine, above Lake Garda

becomes a path, climbing steeply through more olive terraces. When you meet the VIA PANORAMICA (❷) again, follow it to the left, rounding a bend, soon walking past the HOTEL BELLAVISTA — at last on an easy gradient. Follow this road, which lives up to its name, passing another fine viewpoint — you can now see up to the little hill on which the Madonna stands. Beside the road is a grassy bank — a fine spot for a break and to enjoy the views (Picnic 15).

You soon come to a junction (**29min**), where you turn left downhill opposite a sign 'VIA

PANORAMICA'. Then take the first turning uphill to the right, beside a small SHRINE and a water point (VIA SANT'ANTONIO). In about seven minutes you meet an asphalt lane. Turn left here, passing a tall old fir tree behind a hedge on the right. Keep straight on where a driveway heads off to the right and ignore a turning 30m further on. After another 50m, at a Y-fork, keep right, up to a house with decorated gates. Take the path alongside this house, going up some metal steps. A fenced path then leads you up a few more steps, to the huge white **Madonna dell'Accoglienza** (❸; **49min**). This statue, protected by graceful Lombardy pines and illuminated at night, was blessed by Pope John Paul II in 1993 and looks beneficently down on Malcesine. A secluded and peaceful spot to enjoy the fine views.

Retrace your steps to the house and then turn left on a marked CYCLE ROUTE. From this narrow path, with its excellent views up to San Michele and the Monte Baldo cable car station (Walk 28), you wind down beside an old farm and more modern houses, always surrounded by olive trees. You meet the end of an asphalt road by an ARCHED SHRINE at **Paier** (❹; **58min**). Turn right uphill along the road. *(But for the Short walk, turn left here.)*

Walk past vines and fruit trees and, in less than one minute, go left on a wide path that climbs steeply to meet the road again. Continue up this road to rejoin the VIA PANORAMICA once more and turn left (**1h05min**). There are now more wonderful views over Malcesine from opposite a SHRINE (the path from San Michele, followed on Alternative walk 28, joins the road here; ❺). Keep on the road, which now contours the hillside. Ignore any signs to Malcesine until, after about 15 minutes, you arrive at **Dumez** (the sign naming this hamlet looks like a street sign; it's on the left, by a bus stop). Ignore Via Palazzina; carry on until you can turn down left down VIA GARDA (❻; **1h21min**).

Descending quite steeply, you reach a house built on a little knoll, with decorative lions dangling light bulbs on the gateposts. The asphalt ends here, and you follow a cobbled track to the right, below the same house and beside a green wire fence. Just around a bend there is another fine view over Malcesine. You meet a cobbled track and carry on, beside an old SHRINE, to a junction where a red/white-waymarked track joins from the right. Follow this track down to an asphalt road near a farm that sells butter and cheese. Carry on to meet a larger road, where you turn left. After passing the car park for the cable car station (❼), you reach the main road in **Malcesine** (**1h52min**).

To return to the bus stop, turn left along the main road. To return to the ferry terminal, go under the subway and then either wander through the maze of streets in the old town or turn left along the main road and then right just befre the ROUNDABOUT (signposted for the port). Follow the signs for parking past the municipal buildings, then take steps opposite the CAR PARK down to the FERRY TERMINAL and PORT (❶; **1h57min**).

Walk 30: DALCO CIRCUIT FROM LIMONE SUL GARDA

See also photograph page 115
Distance/time: 7.7km/4.8mi; 3h23min
Grade: ● strenuous, mainly on steep mountain paths; ascent/ descent 850m/2790ft . You must be sure-footed and have a head for heights, especially in the Pura Valley. Various waymarked routes
Equipment: see page 26. Walking poles. Refreshments are available at Limone sul Garda; nothing (and no water) en route.
Transport: to Limone sul Garda (Car tour 5); (paid) parking near the starting point (45° 48.828'N, 10° 47.577'E). Or (recommended, as bus service is very limited)
Nearest accommodation: Limone sul Garda, Riva del Garda or Torbole
Short walk: Valle del Singol. 4.3km/2.6mi; 1h10min. ● Easy; walking shoes will suffice. Access as above. Follow the main walk to a picnic table shortly before the 40min-point (4). A path on the right here, by a fence, leads down to an open area by the river. Then retrace your steps to Limone.

Limone sul Garda, one of the most popular resorts on the western shores of the lake, has a charming old town centred around a small fishing harbour. It is probably named after the lemon tree that, from the 15th century onwards, created great prosperity in this area. The unusual columns of the lemon houses, still seen on the terraced hillsides, are the remains of this ancient industry. Our walk takes you up the peaceful and beautiful Valle del Singol, a natural gateway to the mountains behind the lake, with tremendous views from the high cliffs above. On the descent, you will see some of the amazing structures which allowed the lemon to flourish further north than it had ever been grown before.

Start the walk at the MAIN BUS STOP (1) in **Limone sul Garda**, just above the CHURCH. Walk up the road opposite, VIA CALDOGNO, at the left of the TOURIST OFFICE. Take the first turn to the right, to quickly meet a cobbled way, VIA MILANESA, where you turn left. Occasional waymarks guide you straight ahead uphill, past the BAR MILANESA; then you cross an old stone BRIDGE over a bubbling stream (2; **18min**).

Carry on up the **Valle del Singol**, soon coming to a notice board in English. You are now entering the Parco Naturale dell'Alto Garda Bresciano. This quiet hinterland seems worlds apart from the busy lakeside, just a few minutes away. You cross a small side stream beside a little waterfall and pass a ruined circular building. Further up there are several dams and a

View over Valle del Singol from near the 1h35min-point in the walk

path signposted to Dalco, which you *ignore* (❸). Hemmed in by high cliffs, the cobbled way is unrelentingly steep. Eventually you reach a junction with another signpost pointing left to DALCO (❹; **40min**).

Follow this narrow path as it zigzags up into the pine woods in the **Valle Scaglione**. Before long you leave the trees, with fine views back across the Valle del Singol, and on a sharp bend you can see Lake Garda for the first time. As you climb you may wonder how the path will negotiate the high cliffs above. Do not worry! The route is easy, although very steep, eventually reaching the top of the cliffs and a CLEARING in the woods (**1h35min**).

From the left of this clearing take the signposted path to DEGA which, for a very pleasant change, is not uphill! In less than four minutes you come to a signposted junction. (Here we recommend that you turn left on a path for a short detour to a superb viewpoint. After about two minutes turn left uphill off this path, to reach the cliff edge — a great place to enjoy a break. Allow about seven minutes return.) Continue on the Dega/Tremosine path (ROUTE 110), through patches of grassland amongst the trees. Just beyond a summer house, beside the ruins of the small CHURCH at **Dalco** (❺; **1h40min**), turn right

uphill. From here a fairly level path takes you near the old houses of **Dega** (6; **1h52min**). In about three minutes, where the path leaves a shallow gully, walk left for good views over the lake and to nearby Monte Bestone.

A minute later you reach another junction with a wooden barrier, where ROUTE 109 joins your path. Follow the signpost for LIMONE/ TREMOSINE, now with excellent, clear views. Below you can see your descent path to Limone sul Garda, as well as the optional extension to Monte Bestone. The path drops quite steeply as it makes its way around the precipitous headwall of **Val Pura**. In one place there is a short section of path protected with a CABLE HANDRAIL — this can be avoided by going to the left. You pass another small round building, then the path continues very easily to a JUNCTION (7; **2h10min**). The main walk turns left here, following ROUTE 123 TO LIMONE SUL GARDA. *(But keep straight on for the optional ascent of Monte Bestone described below.)*

The path descends into Val Pura on an easy gradient. It is rather loose and stony, but the good views down the valley make up for the discomfort underfoot. You meet the stream bed, where you walk first on one side and then on the other. Three minutes after crossing the stream for the last time, you reach a WATER STATION. From here continue down a concrete road, to meet an asphalt road (8; **3h01min**).

Take the lower road on the left by the first houses on the outskirts of Limone sul Garda. Go past some large new houses set amidst the old olive terraces, to come to a junction. Continue straight on, passing the birthplace of Daniele Comboni, founder of the Missionari Comboniani (missionaries in Africa). Above you will see some of the old lemon houses.* Just after the missionary's house, keep right downhill, soon passing another road that joins from the right. In nine minutes you reach a large junction. Turn left along VIA FOL, to cross the stream. At the next junction turn right downhill to return to the main road, opposite the BUS STOP in **Limone sul Garda** (**3h23min**).

Optional ascent of Monte Bestone (allow 55min return and an additional 240m of ascent/ descent). At the JUNCTION (7; 2h10min), keep straight on along the wide path for about 250m, passing one small path to the left, and then turn left down a very narrow path, which is *not* clearly waymarked. The descent is unexpected, but soon you traverse the hillside. In about four minutes there is a fine viewpoint across Lake Garda. Continue on to a small grassy area, where you may encounter hunters during the shooting season (see Nuisances, page 28). Cross this clearing diagonally to the right, then take a narrow, steeply climbing path. A little higher up, the path becomes much better defined and affords wonderful views. After about 18 minutes of hard climbing you reach two crosses on the SUMMIT of **Monte Bestone** (9), where you are rewarded by uninterrupted views (described on page 116).

---

*Each consisted of four high pillars placed to form a 7m square, with low, dense-foliage citrus in front and a mature lemon tree bearing up to 600 fruits a year in the middle. This was secured to the pillars to prevent wind damage. Another fruit tree was trained along the back wall. These 'houses' formed continuous lines along the terraces. Commercial production ended some 50 years ago; only a few trees and pillars remain.

Walk 31: MONTE BESTONE

Distance/time: 2.5km/1.6mi; 1h07min
Grade: ● easy, with about 200m/656ft of ascent/descent
Equipment: see page 26. Refreshments are available at Voltino.
Transport: 🚗 Follow Car tour 5 from Riva del Garda through Limone sul Garda to Voltino, then turn right for Campi (a few metres before the church). Wind up this road, past houses, to the Hotel Balze (45° 47.277'N, 10° 45.909'E). Park beside the road or drive up to the hotel and through the main car park, beyond which there seems to be no objection to parking.
Nearest accommodation: Limone sul Garda, Riva del Garda or Torbole

The ridge to the summit of Monte Bestone affords one of the best outlooks over Lake Garda. It is an ideal short walk to include in a day of touring the Tremosine plateau. Little climbing is involved, and the views are magnificent.

Start out at the HOTEL BALZE (❶): walk through the hotel complex, past the TENNIS COURTS. Opposite some chalets, take a narrow path on the left (behind a low wire fence), signposted 'NO 11 DELLA ROCCA'. You rise up through scrubby trees, to reach a broad ridge with fine views. Continue along the ridge, perhaps exploring the side paths to viewpoints (Picnic 16), before descending a

View over Limone sul Garda from near Monte Bestone (Picnic 16)

little way to a small COL (❷; **22min**) where a path (ROUTE 12) goes left. *(Take this path for the Alternative return below.)*

Carry straight on, climbing easily on a good path, to the summit of **Monte Bestone** (❸; **37min**) — a spectacular vantage point. The birds-eye view over Limone sul Garda is superb, and you are treated to uninterrupted views up and down Lake Garda — it is so wide at its southern end that you feel you are looking out to sea. On the far side is Monte Baldo, while to the north, at the head of the lake, lies Torbole, with Monte Stivo (Walk 27) prominent beyond. To the southwest is the beautiful green plateau of Tremosine.

To make the most of the superlative views, we suggest that you return the same way to the HOTEL BALZE (❶; **1h07min**). However, if you prefer a circuit, see below.

Alternative return (adds 5-10min): Retrace your steps back to the COL at the 22min-point (❷) and turn right down a path through the trees (ROUTE 12). After five minutes, keep right at a junction (waymarked). You soon come to a small farm where you join an asphalt driveway (do not be deterred by the 'Private' signs; it is a waymarked route). Continue down to meet a road and turn left, soon passing a tennis centre and the HOTEL CAMPI. Just beyond is the HOTEL BALZE (❶).

Walk 32: PASSO NOTA CIRCUIT FROM VESIO

See map opposite and photograph on page 24
Distance/time: 18.5km/11.5mi; 4h53min
Grade: ● moderate; a long walk on gravel and asphalt roads and tracks, with about 900m/2952ft of ascent/descent
Equipment: see page 26. Refreshments are available at the *rifugio* at Passo Nota.
Transport: Follow Car tour 5 to Vesio. On a sharp left-hand bend before entering the village proper, turn right, towards 'Passo Nota' and 'Campi'. At the top of the hill turn right and, at the crossroads, go right — to a large picnicking and parking area (45° 47.645'N, 10° 44.876'E).
from Limone sul Garda to Vesio; see 'Transport information' inside the back cover. From the bus stop allow six minutes to reach the start of the walk: walk up Via Orsino and, at a junction above a children's play area, turn left and walk up to a crossroads. Turn right here, passing a small picnic area, to reach a large car park where the walk begins.
Nearest accommodation: Limone sul Garda, Riva del Garda, Torbole
***Short walk:* Alveo Lago Bondo circuit.** 3.7km/2.3mi; 50min.
● Easy, with gentle ups and downs, one rise of just 30m/100ft; trainers will suffice. Access as above. *If you come by car* (1), walk back towards the centre of the village by turning left at the crossroads and then right at the next junction, just above a children's play area. Go down the slope, to pass the BUS STOP (a); *start here if you come by bus.* Walk through the village on the cobbled road, passing HOTEL SOLE. Watch for a SUNDIAL on a house, and turn right between this house and a *bar-tabacceria*. The narrow road climbs behind houses and goes under a stone archway, the PONTE ANGELO CAVAZZA. Turn left at the top and continue up to a road junction. Go straight across on VIA DELLE GLERE, keeping right on a gravel track and ignoring a signposted path to Piazzolo. Carry on along the track that overlooks the cultivated land in the bed *(alveo)* of the one-time lake, **Lago Bondo**. The track eventually bends to the right in front of a large dairy farm, to come to a junction. Turn right here, soon crossing a river bed (usually dry). Walk on to an ASPHALT ROAD (8) and turn right, now following the main walk back to the CAR PARK (1) above Vesio.

This walk uses one of the old military roads to access the head of the Bondo Valley at Passo Nota, an important junction deep within the mountains. Some of the worst fighting in the First World War, between the Austrians and the Italians, took place in this area — a scenario difficult to envisage as you explore this serene valley.

Start the walk at the large CAR PARK (1) just above **Vesio**, at the beginning of **Valle di Bondo**. Walk away from the village, then take the gravel track straight ahead, VIA G ANGELINI (named for the man responsible for the re-afforestation of this area after World War I). The track turns left after only a few metres, by a sign for PASSO NOTA. After 12 minutes the track goes past a MEMORIAL to the forester, Giulio Angelini. You can walk up the steps of this tall monument to look across the Bondo Valley.
The track climbs through trees at an easy gradient, in a series of

zigzags. On two of the bends you are treated to good views over the valley and the Tremosine plateau to the south. You climb steadily and, after about 50 minutes, pass a path off right to Bocca dei Sospiri (**1h02min**), which is just above. From here, the ascent is much more gentle, and the thinning trees allow some fine views across the valley and up to the mountain at its head, Corno della Marogna. After another 22 minutes ignore a track off to the right and then, 20 minutes later, pass a small cairn indicating a path down to the Bondo Valley.

In a further 15 minutes you reach the first of a series of TUNNELS (❷; **1h59min**) — these are short and you do not need a torch. You soon start to see reminders of the First World War — dugouts and little tunnels. Here the way, now no more than a wide path, is just on the edge of the steepening valley, with tremendous views to the rock towers of Corno della Marogna in the northwest.

About two minutes after the sixth and FINAL TUNNEL (❸), you come to a SIGNPOSTED JUNCTION (❹). (*Do* take a short 12-minute return detour here, to a wonderful viewpoint and splendid spot for a break. Turn right on a narrow path and, after a short climb, turn left at a T-junction. Walk up past a small cabin, to a little KNOLL (ⓑ). From this point you can see over Valle del Singol all the way down to Limone sul Garda.)

The main walk continues along the wide path and, with the climbing all but done, you contour around the hillside. Pass another fine viewpoint beside a pylon and soon begin to descend, now on a track again. Ignore one path to the left and then, two minutes later, another to the right, to reach a large cattle shed (**Stalla Val Cerese**; ❺; **2h45min**). A little further on you come to a small sign to the 'CIMITERO'. Follow this for a few metres, up into a grassy glade where, set amidst pine trees, you will find a small WWI CEMETERY (❻; **2h55min**). An intricate barbed wire fence encloses it, with symbolic barbed wire crosses on the entrance gates. Just above the cemetery is a trench and concrete battlements — a good place for a break with views over to Cima Pari, which stands above Lago di Ledro.

Return to the track and, in only five minutes, you reach a junction at **Passo Nota** (❼; **3h02min**). Above and behind a large wartime gun stands the **Rifugio Passo Nota**, where you can buy drinks and refreshments. Turn left at this junction, passing signposts and a map. Here fork left down the gravel road, which soon gains an asphalt surface. You walk below the rock towers of **Corno della Marogna**, passing a turn for the Rifugio Pedercini.

The easy, winding descent leads past a large picnic area (**3h55min**). Keep on down this attractive road, passing dams on the small river and more picnic tables. After about 18 minutes the road crosses the river and, in a further 12 minutes, the valley widens and you reach fertile farmland with belled cows, fields of corn and meadows full of wild flowers. Ignore a ROAD ON THE RIGHT (❽). *(The Short walk joins here.)* Soon after, you pass a small sand and gravel quarry, before climbing the NATURAL DAM of the **Alveo Lago Bondo**. At a crossroads, turn left, to quickly regain the CAR PARK above **Vesio** (❶; **4h53min**).

Walk 33: MONTE CASTELLO

Distance/time: 3.3km/1mi; 1h
Grade: easy; a steep but short climb on an asphalt road and then on good (but somewhat exposed) paths, with 230m/750ft of ascent/descent overall.
Equipment: see page 26. Trainers will suffice. Refreshments are available at the Santuario Madonna di Montecastello.
Transport: Follow Car tour 5 to Tignale or, more directly, drive south from Riva del Garda through Limone sul Garda and past Campione del Garda. About 7km south of Campione, turn right to Tignale and drive up to and through this large village. Park at the top of the pass, about 1.5km beyond Tignale and below Monte Castello (45° 44.533'N, 10° 43.826'E). to the car park below Monte Castello; see 'Transport information' inside the back cover.
Nearest accommodation: Gargnano or Limone sul Garda
Short walk: Madonna di Montecastello. 1.5km/1mi; 27min. Grade, equipment and access as above. Follow the main walk up to the Santuario and then return the same way. The motor road is currently closed to vehicles.

One of the most famous places of worship on Lake Garda is the Santuario Madonna di Montecastello, which stands on the edge of sheer cliffs high above the lake. Built upon the ruins of an ancient castle, this church has a hermitage beside it that attracts thousands of pilgrims every year. We take you up to and beyond these sacred buildings, along a ridge (somewhat exposed in places) with superb views. A final, easy descent makes this a delightful circular walk.

Begin by the CHAPEL at the end of the CAR PARK (1): walk up the road, VIA DON DOMENICO TRIBOLDI. You pass attractively painted shrines depicting scenes from the New Testament. There are two pedestrian short cuts and a stepped pavement, where the road (currently closed to motor vehicles) is particularly steep. At length you reach a painted archway, which leads into a small car park, with the **Santuario Madonna di Montecastello** and hermitage beyond (2; **15min**). There is also a bar and a toilet here. Walk through the old metal gates and up the imposing steps to the church, which although plain on the outside has a richly decorated interior. From the parapet you can look down over 2000ft of almost sheer cliffs to Lake Garda — quite a spectacle! To continue, follow the signposted path below and to the left of the church and hermitage, passing under a modern extension. From here a path takes you up past SMALL CAVES, reminders of wartime activity in this area. After 10 minutes you come to a wonderful viewpoint, where you can look back over the rooftops of the hermitage and church, down to Lake Garda. An even better VIEWPOINT on a rocky outcrop is reached just a minute later (3; **26min**; Picnic 17). Take care: the cliff edge is unprotected.

Top: Santuario Madonna di Montecastello, from the last viewpoint on the cliffs; below: the sanctuary from the rocky outcrop at the 26min-point (Picnic 17)

Carry on up the path, with superb views all the way, passing a LOOKOUT TUNNEL. You come to further viewpoint, on the right of the path, set amongst a few pine trees — another sheer drop down to the lake. Here, leave the main path by turning left up a narrower path, to a gun emplacement surmounted by a large CROSS, the SUMMIT of **Monte Castello** (4; **33min**).

Continue past the cross for a few metres and then bear right, to drop down to the main path again, where you turn left. Follow this as it traverses the hillside, passing many dugouts. After eight minutes you reach a somewhat vertiginous FINAL VIEWPOINT (5; **41min**; photograph left). From here you can see the impressive situation of the church, perched just at the edge of the cliffs. In the other direction there is a fine view over the Tremosine plateau and up the lake to Riva del Garda and Torbole.

The walk now turns left around the hillside, to join a waymarked path on the left. Follow this downhill to another junction, reached in only one minute. Go straight on here, *leaving* the waymarks; the clear path descends gently. After four minutes you come to another junction, where more waymarks guide you to the right. Quickly coming to a T-junction, turn left. Continue down this path and, as you descend, look back for a lovely view over the hillside village of Prabione. When the path meets the road after eight minutes, turn left to return to the CAR PARK and BUS STOP (1; **1h**).

Walk 34: MONTE CASTELLO DI GAINO

Distance/time: 5km/3mi; 2h05min

Grade: moderate. Mainly on narrow — sometimes exposed — — forest paths, with a total ascent/descent of 390m/1280ft. You will need to use your hands on the final few metres to the summit, where there is a fixed rope.

Equipment: see page 26. Walking poles. Refreshments are available at Navazzo. Waymarked route 21

Transport: From Riva del Garda drive south through Limone sul Garda and past Campioni del Garda to pick up Car tour 5 about 4km north of Gargnano, where you turn right and drive up to Navazzo. Park on the far side of the village just beyond the bus stop (45° 41.086'N, 10° 38.019'E). to Navazzo; see 'Transport information' inside the back cover.

Nearest accommodation: Gargnano, Limone sul Garda

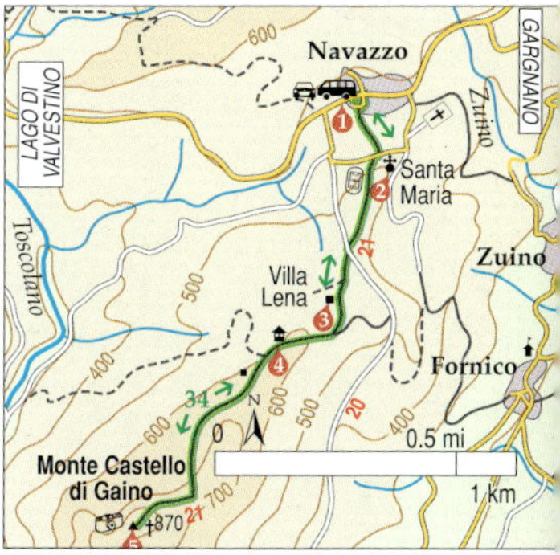

The little peak of Monte Castello di Gaino is clearly visible and looks very inviting as you drive up to Navazzo. The exertion needed to reach the summit is more than rewarded by the superlative views. This is another short walk that can easily be included in a day's outing, or when time is limited.

Start the walk at the CAR PARK or BUS STOP (1): walk back into the centre of **Navazzo**. In the small *piazza,* just past the fountain, turn right along a narrow asphalt road. Follow this out of the village and then through fields, towards a church. Look right as you approach the church, to see the three tops of Monte Castello di Gaino. Go up the steps to the church of **Santa Maria** (2; **5min**); the porch has a fine painted ceiling. Follow the sign for MONTE CASTELLO, to the right. A track takes you uphill past a FOOTBALL PITCH.

Higher up the track becomes a path, before a short descent brings you to a track junction (**15min**). Go straight across on a cart track, quickly forking left at another junction signposted to MONTE CASTELLO. You soon come to yet another junction opposite the grounds of VILLA LENA (3). Here you keep right and follow the waymarked route gently uphill past a CLEARING WITH A HUNTER'S HIDE, where you reach the ridge (4; **29min**). Now follow a path skirting to the right of the ridge through thick woodland (*take care* near a CONCRETE SHELTER dug into the hillside — the path passes very close to its collapsed roof).

After 30 minutes you regain the ridge briefly, but there are no views. The path goes to the right again, contouring and climbing easily to the bottom of the final steep section of the ascent. A rope has been fixed to the trees and rocks, affording security as you scramble towards the top. You emerge from the trees just a few metres below the SUMMIT of **Monte Castello di Gaino** (5; **1h13min**), which is marked by a large CROSS. Nearby is a book in

Above: Monte Castello di Gaino, from the road to Navazzo; left: view north over Lake Garda from the summit

which you can record your visit for posterity!

The views from the top are marvellous, all the way down to the southern end of Lake Garda, with Sirmione on its long and narrow peninsula clearly visible. Directly to the west is the bulk of neighbouring Monte Pizzocolo and, to the right of this, Valvestino (visited during Car tour 5) and Monte Caplone (Walk 35). Gargnano is directly below and, across the lake, is the long dominant ridge of Monte Baldo (Walk 28).

Return along your outward route to **Navazzo** (**2h05min**).

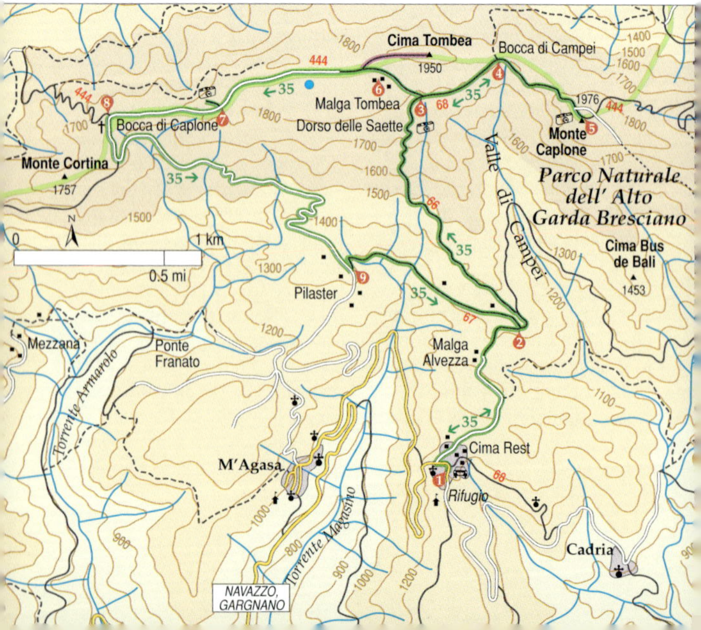

Walk 35: MONTE CAPLONE

See map opposite
Distance/time: 17km/10.5mi; 5h13min
Grade: ● strenuous; mainly on good tracks and old military roads, with an overall ascent/descent of 800m/2625ft. Easily followed, waymarked routes
Equipment: see page 26. Refreshments are available at Cima Rest.
Transport: 🚗 Following Car tour 5, turn right at the 66.5km-point towards M'Agasa. At the entrance to this village turn sharp right and take the narrow road to Cima Rest. Park in the car park near the bar (45° 46.866'N, 10° 37.762'E).
Nearest accommodation: Gargnano, Limone sul Garda

Shorter walk: Malga Tombea and Bocca di Caplone. 12.3km/ 7.6mi; 3h55min. ● Moderate, with an ascent/descent of 650m/ 2130ft; equipment and access as above. Follow the main walk to the 1h37min-point at ❸ and turn left to the farm buildings of **Malga Tombea** (❻). Then follow the main walk from the 3h-point to the end.

What a fine mountain walk this is! From the attractive hamlet of Cima Rest, you walk up past traditional steep-roofed hay barns and on to the high summer grazings of Cima Tombea amidst a great variety and proliferation of wild flowers. Monte Caplone has many faces, the easily gained summit contrasting with the sheer cliffs, dramatic spurs and spires seen on the approach.

Starting from the CAR PARK near the bar in **Cima Rest** (❶), walk back up the road and, just before a little CHAPEL, turn right at a large signpost for CAPLONE. Follow this concreted road through the fields and then steeply uphill, past some old farm buildings, to reach **Malga Alvezza**, a scattering of houses. From here the track descends a short way, before climbing again to a SIGNPOSTED JUNCTION (❷; **34min**). Keep right uphill to come to another signpost in about one minute, where you take the red/white waymarked path to the left, again signposted to CAPLONE (ROUTE 66).

At first you climb gently through upland grazings and later through the thickening trees. After about 24 minutes the path begins to zigzag, as the ground gets steeper, before it crosses a small stream. The views improve as you climb, and you can see across to the nearby villages with their tightly clustered houses. The path escapes from the trees and goes up to the right of a small fenced area, beyond which you join a faint track. Monte Caplone is now straight ahead, presenting its steepest side. The track becomes more distinct as it continues up to a MAJOR TRACK JUNCTION (❸; **1h37min**). *(The Shorter walk turns left here.)*

Turn right downhill, quickly passing a botanical INFORMATION BOARD. Follow the track around the side of **Cima Tombea**, renowned for its wonderful flora. You cross the head of the steep-sided **Valle di Campei**, with cliffs above and below. At one point this old military road (SENTIERO ANTONIOLI) passes beneath a rock arch. Your route continues up to a COL, the **Bocca di Campei** (❹; **1h58min**), where you turn your back on the great views to the north and climb a path (way-marked but not signed) towards Monte Caplone.

The way is quite easy but, on the narrow path, you may have to use your hands in places. From the

Approaching Monte Caplone

SUMMIT of **Monte Caplone** (❺; **2h14min**), the views are far-reaching and breathtaking. Lake Garda and Monte Baldo are easily seen, as are many hills to the south and west, but it is the northern view that is most dramatic — the Brenta Dolomites and Adamello Alps stand out distinctly on the horizon, above the nearby peaks.

Return from here to the JUNCTION (❸) first encountered at the 1h37min-point and carry straight on. The old military road, little more than a track, passes behind the farm buildings of **Malga Tombea** (**3h**). Keep on this wide track, which traverses the hillside — excellent summer pastures — taking time to look back to the summit of Cima Tombea, which if you have time, is an easy — pathless — climb.

Beyond a large POOL, the road starts to descend gently and you come to another signpost. Here it is possible to cut up to the ridge on the right, to another fine VIEWPOINT (❼) to the north. Carry on, passing many DUGOUTS hewn from the solid rock, to eventually reach **Bocca di Caplone** (❽; **3h31min**). Beside the junction on this wide col is a pretty Madonna, a memorial to a well-loved *padre*.

Ignore the other tracks and stay on the main military road, which descends to the left. As you wend your way downhill there is ample time to admire the views to the south. Lower down you again meet trees and, at the top of a second series of zigzags, the road becomes concreted. At the big bend to the right, ignore the track off left (it *may* be signed to Il Bait). About 40 minutes from Bocca di Caplone you reach a SIGNPOSTED JUNCTION on the outskirts of **Pilaster** (❾; **4h24min**). Here you must double back to the left and, after two minutes, cross a stream. Continue along this track, to come to open pasture and go by farm buildings. An easy uphill slope will bring you back to the junction you first met at the 34min-point (❷; **4h47min**). Here turn right, to retrace your steps to **Cima Rest** (❶; **5h13min**).

Walk 36: MOERNA CIRCUIT VIA BOCCA COCCA

See also photograph page 29
Distance/time: 14.6km/9mi; 4h19min
Grade: ●❢ technically easy, but a long walk with an ascent/descent of 800m/2625ft. Vertiginous path sections currently well protected. Well signed and waymarked
Equipment: see page 26. Refreshments available at Moerna, Persone
Transport: 🚗 Follow Car tour 5 and park in the car park below the little cemetery at Moerna (45° 45.489'N, 10° 34.811'E).
Nearest accommodation: Gargnano, Limone sul Garda
***Short walk*: Bocca Cocca.** 6km/3.7mi; 1h40min. ● Easy, with an ascent/descent of 350m/1150ft); access as above. Trainers are adequate. Follow the main walk to **Bocca Cocca** (❷)and back.

We found this wonderful walk quite by chance and what a find it turned out to be! Fifty years ago there were no motorable roads in this area, and a restful tranquillity still prevails. The small villages, with their tightly clustered houses, were built to allow as much fertile land as possible to be used for agriculture. One such charming village, Moerna, is at the start of this easy walk, which takes you to a splendid outlook above Lake Idro. There then follows a fine mountainside traverse, where you can enjoy magnificent views over picturesque countryside, with Monte Caplone (Walk 35) as a dramatic backdrop.

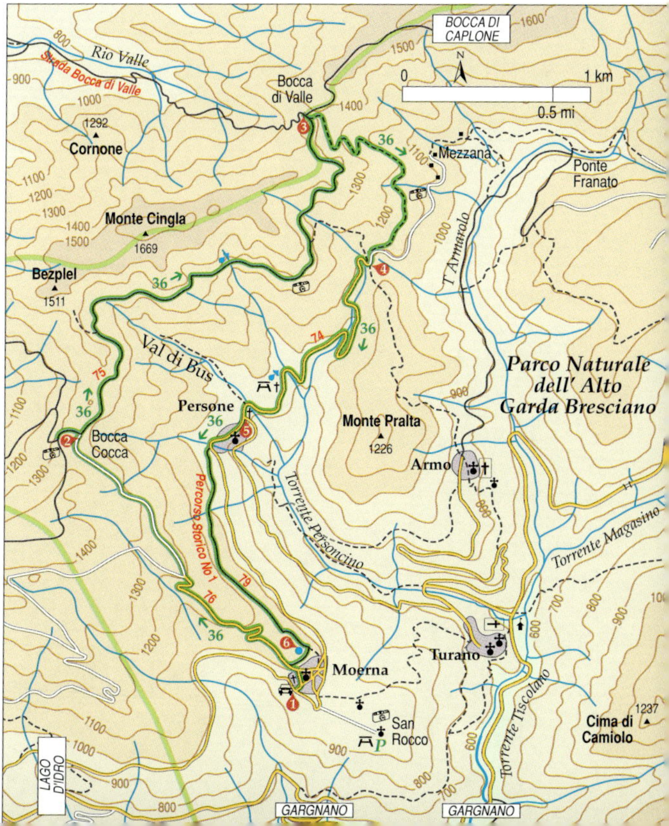

Start out from the CAR PARK (❶) and walk up to the little CEMETERY in **Moerna**. Pick up an asphalt road that rises along the right-hand side of the cemetery, passing a signpost for BOCCA COCCA. Continue up this road between old terraces, with good views over the wooded hills to the south. Keep on this road to a SIGNPOSTED JUNCTION (**31min**), where the tar runs out. Go right here, enjoying views of Monte Caplone and, nearer at hand, Monte Cingla (later, you will walk under its cliffs). The track gradually climbs to another signpost. Keep to the right here — above is a hunter's cabin (see Nuisances, page 28). Just a minute later you reach the col of **Bocca Cocca** (❷; **55min**). If you walk around the barrier and

Monte Caplone from above Mezzana

a short way down the other side, you have a lovely view over Lake Idro. *(The Short walk returns from here.)*

From the col, take the signposted path to BOCCA DI VALLE (to the left if you are looking back towards Moerna). This narrow path traverses the mountainside, keeping below the ridge and affording some marvellous views. After about 17 minutes, keep right at a fork and soon escape the trees to round the steep head of **Val di Bus**. This next section is very dramatic and amazingly scenic. You pass by the limestone rock towers and beneath the crags and sometimes-overhanging cliffs of **Monte Cingla**, while below are the clustered rooftops of Persone.

After about 25 minutes, look out for a small SPRING within a shallow hole in the base of one of the cliffs (**1h40min**). The path now becomes quite narrow in places, but wooden railings have been placed along the most vertiginous stretches. In another 12 minutes you round a bend to see Monte Caplone and, to its right, the serrated ridge of Cima Bus de Bali. Dotted across the high summer grazings are small houses and hay barns. The terrain becomes more wooded and, as the path continues traversing, there are several small ups and downs. You reach a sign-posted junction just below the tree-shrouded **Bocca di Valle** (❸; **2h 27min**). Unfortunately all views from here down to the valleys are obscured — only the distant mountains are visible.

Ignore the path from the col to Bocca di Caplone and return to the junction just below, where you turn left. This is *not* a waymarked route, but there should be a sign in a tree for 'MESSANE', which may refer to the houses below at Mezzana. This path descends in wide easy zigzags, before traversing out of the steep and thickly wooded valley on the right, to emerge beside an old derelict building. An incredibly peaceful scene opens out before you — no cars, only the sound of tinkling cow bells.

The path gradually widens into a track — you can amble along appreciating the views. If you look up, you will see the precipitous mountainside which you have just traversed. Go by a new house with a very steep roof and soon come to an asphalt road on a small COL (❹; **3h03min**).

Turn right along this quiet road and begin to descend towards Persone. After about 24 minutes you come to a water point, picnic table and a pretty painted SHRINE atop a small incline. Continue past another SHRINE and reach a junction just below **Persone** (❺; **3h33min**).

Turn right and walk up into this compact cluster of houses. There is an interesting information board, with explanations in English, about this attractive village and its environs. Continue along the road, passing the CHURCH, to leave Persone. In five minutes, on a left-hand bend, take the signposted path to the right — 'PERCORSO STORICO NO. 1'. This 'historical' path is waymarked, although at rather distant intervals, and climbs quite steeply through trees for about 20 minutes, before levelling off and traversing the hillside towards Moerna.

Eventually you come to a grassy area and a POND (❻; **4h10min**). Turn right here, around the pond, to find a cobbled track signposted to CAPOVALLE. Follow this track to reach the asphalt road along which you started the walk. Turn left to return to the CAR PARK at **Moerna** (❶; **4h19min**).

Walk 37: ROCCHETTA GIOCHELLO CIRCUIT

Distance/time: 10.4km/6.5mi; 4h30min

Grade: ●❢ very strenuous, with a steep and unrelenting ascent of 1125m/3690ft and an equally steep descent. Paths are mainly good, but some are exposed and the only (cable) protection is at the summit. The descent is steep and skiddy, sometimes on loose gravel. You must be sure-footed and have a head for heights. Good waymarking and signposting

Equipment: see page 26. Walking poles; ***torch*** to explore the wartime entrenchments mentioned below.

Refreshments are available at Biacesa.

Transport: 🚗 From Riva del Garda (Car tour 5) follow road signs for Lago di Ledro. Approximately 1km after the long tunnel, park in the large car park at the left of the road just before Biacesa (45° 51.904'N, 10° 48.445'E). 🚌 from Riva del Garda to Biacesa; see 'Transport information' inside the back cover. You *must* keep an eye on your watch; walking times will be very tight!

Nearest accommodation: Riva del Garda, Torbole

From the ridge crest of Rocchetta Giochello, the scenic grandeur of the crenellated towers and the magnificence of the limestone cliffs which drop precipitously down to Riva del Garda is breathtaking. The awesome display of nature on this mountain makes the arduous climb and descent through trees fade into insignificance.

Begin at the CAR PARK (❶) and walk up the busy main road to the BUS STOP in **Biacesa**. Here turn right up VIA DEL DAZI; there are signposts on the wall opposite for the red/white waymarked ROUTE 417. Halfway up the street, on a bend, keep straight ahead. At the T-junction, turn right, still on ROUTE 417, which you stay on all the way to Rocchetta Giochello. The well-waymarked and signposted route climbs out of the village on a cobbled road, past houses and through vineyards, with views up to the cliffs of Rocchetta. Follow route 417 through a series of forks and junctions; the cobbled road becomes a path that soon enters woodland.

At a junction (❷; **38min**) ignore route 460 forking off to the right. (Route 460 leads to the church of San Giovanni and to Rocca, an Austrian stronghold in WWI; some of the emplacements have been restored and may be visited.) Keep left and follow the path steadily uphill; it gradually narrows as it gains height. At the 1000m contour, you reach another junction (**1h18min**). Keep straight on here and climb

even more steeply in the upper **Val Vasotina**, occasionally having to use your hands. At one point the path goes beneath a small overhanging cliff, from where there are good views across the steep craggy hillside and up to Cima Valdes, the slightly higher neighbour of Rocchetta Giochello. The SPRING (3) that you pass, on your right, is the only source of water on this route.

Eventually you reach a ridge and another junction at a thinly wooded col, the **Bochet dei Concoli** (4; **1h47min**). Turn left and walk along the signposted **Sentiero Rino Zanotti** (still ROUTE 417) beneath the crest of the ridge. Soon you can see back to Biacesa — a long way down! After about eight minutes you reach the ridge again, at a superb VIEWPOINT. There are few vantage points on this ridge, so we recommend this as an excellent place for a break. Below you, and we mean *directly* below, are the rooftops of Riva del Garda, viewed as if from an aeroplane. Beyond are Torbole and Monte Brione (Walk 25), shaped like the

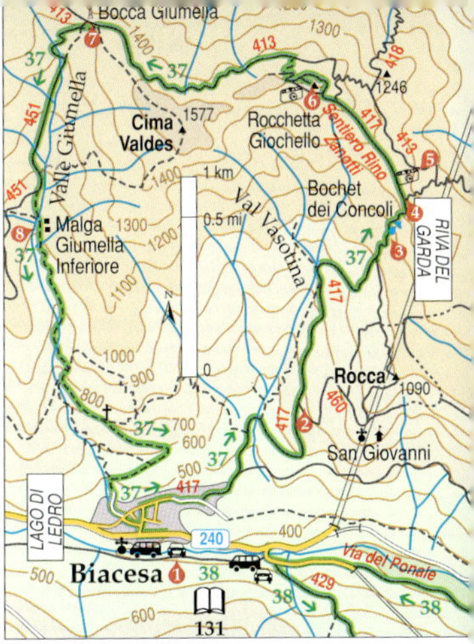

Rocchetta from Torbole (above) and from Nodice (below)

segments of an orange. To the north of these lies Arco with its fairytale castle (Walk 26) and, as a backdrop, the peak of Monte Stivo (Walk 27). To the southwest, above Malcesine, is the long ridge of Monte Baldo (Walk 28).

Continue along the ridge, crossing the crest several times. Along the way you will see remains of WAR-TIME ENTRENCHMENTS, lookout posts, gun emplacements and dugout shelters. The path follows several of the stone-built trenches as you steadily climb. After about 25 minutes you come to a 'PANORAMIC' VIEWPOINT (5), which lives up to its name. Just after this you walk through an OBSERVATION POINT and clamber over more fortifications. Below the summit of Rocchetta Giochello there is a signposted junction (**2h32min**), where you carry on up to the left. A few metres further on, there is another fork where you go right (both left and right options are waymarked). Climb steeply and quickly to another superb viewpoint. Here the path turns sharp left and passes in front of a large dugout under the actual summit. It then bends to the left and climbs from a STONE-BUILT TRENCH to finally reach the TOP of **Rocchetta Giochello** (6; **2h45min**). From here you can imagine this mountain as a bastion in wartime — there are trenches and dugouts everywhere.

The walk now returns the few metres to the trench and then continues along the grassy ridge. In less than two minutes you turn right, following waymarks onto the heavily wooded northern slopes of the ridge. These waymarks soon end, but you quickly fork right at a junction and then drop down in zigzags to meet a well waymarked path. Follow this (ROUTE 413) to the left as it traverses the hillside, sometimes climbing and then gently descending. At one point you near the crest of the ridge once more, but you then drop steeply to **Bocca Giumella** (7; **3h11min**), a wide grassy col, which is easily distinguished by an electricity PYLON.

Take a little path and go under the electricity cables, to reach a small building, from where a wide, well-waymarked path descends (ROUTE 451). The way down is steep and sometimes loose, but it is quite straightforward; however, you *do* need to look out for one junction. You reach this after about 22 minutes, by a sign pointing back up to Bocca Giumella. Just below is a grassy clearing. You *leave* the waymarks now, by forking left above the clearing and dropping down to the ruined buildings of **Malga Giumella Inferiore** (8; **3h41min**).

From the buildings the way continues, still very steep and with a loose surface. Ignore the many red paint marks you see, and go straight downhill. After about 18 minutes the path becomes wider and the surface more secure, as you walk around two steep bends between rocky outcrops. At an attractive SHRINE (**4h08min**) you can rest awhile on the benches, while looking down to Biacesa.

Follow the now-wide path and, after about 11 minutes, ignore any arrows that lead off left. You reach **Biacesa** and, at the asphalt road, go straight across along VIA DELLE BUSE, keeping downhill to a T-junction. Turn right to return to the main road beside the BUS STOP or, if you have driven, walk the short distance down the main road back to the CAR PARK (1; **4h30min**).

Walk 38: NODICE CIRCUIT FROM BIACESA

See also photograph page 129
Distance/time: 7.8km/4.8mi; 2h35min
Grade: ● ! moderate; mainly on good paths and country roads, but with an initial steep climb and an overall ascent/descent of 575m/ 1886ft; well waymarked
Equipment: see page 26. Walking poles. Refreshments are available at Biacesa and Pregasina.
Transport: 🚗 From Riva del Garda (Car tour 5) follow signs for Lago di Ledro. Park at the junction for Pregasina, just after leaving the tunnel (45° 51.870'N, 25° 41.155'E). 🚌 as Walk 37 (page 128) to the Pregasina junction; only one bus a day
Nearest accommodation: Riva del Garda, Torbole

Short walk: Nodice from Pregasina. 4.2km/2.6mi; 1h19min. ● ! Easy-moderate, with an ascent/ descent of 335m; equipment as above. Access: 🚗 as above, but continue to Pregasina and park in the small car park below the church (45° 51.032'N, 10° 49.450'E). **Start** from the CAR PARK in **Pregasina**: walk up the cobbled path and turn left by the old washing area, to pass the CHURCH and continue along a gravel road. At a signposted junction to NODICE, bear right up a very steep concrete road. This becomes a gravel track and then a path. After about 20 minutes fork right at a signposted junction and in another seven minutes (at the top of a rocky gully) pass a fine VIEWPOINT/PICNIC SPOT (5). Rise to another JUNCTION (4). The waymarked path goes left, but you take the path to the *right*, signposted 'ALLA SCALA SANTA'. (Vertigo sufferers may prefer to take the waymarked route up to the COL (2) above and follow the main walk from the 55min-point; then return the same way.) This path traverses below

The Scala Santa steps on Nodice

cliffs and goes through a cleft in the rocks, before climbing the steps shown above, the **Scala Santa**. At the top, climb up a rough path and then turn left along a wide rocky ledge, to reach a balcony VIEWPOINT just below the SUMMIT of **Nodice** (3), with a dugout shelter behind it. Return by retracing your steps or carry straight on along a narrow path edging the cliff. This descends past dugouts to a metal CROSS and MEMORIAL. Keep straight ahead for a few metres, to join the main path at a COL (2). Turn left and walk down to the 'Scala Santa' junction, to retrace your steps to **Pregasina**.

This must be one of the most interesting and exhilarating walks within easy distance of the lakeside resorts. You climb up steps hewn from the rock face, to reach a superb viewpoint on Nodice, a hill scarred by wartime activity. The descent is though the peaceful village of Pregasina and along the old, disused road that winds down towards Lake Garda.

Start at the JUNCTION (❶) east of **Biacesa**; walk towards PREGASINA for about 200m, crossing the **Torrente Ponale**, to find a signposted path to NODICE (ROUTE 429). Take this, climbing sharply up into the trees on your right. After about 20 minutes, fork left, following clear waymarks. The very steep final climb brings you to a signpost at a wooded COL (**Bocca da Lé**). *Ignore* this sign; carry straight on and in about 20m you will come to some WAYMARKED BOULDERS (❷; **55min**).

Turn left to find a war MEMORIAL and a large wartime dugout. On a rock above the memorial is a poignant CROSS built from war refuse. Climb up behind this cross, then take a little path with RED DOTS WAYMARKS that heads to the right, up past a smaller dugout. Continue on by a ruined lookout — inscribed in the concrete is '1915'. Keep to the right and above the cliff edge, to reach a VIEWPOINT just below the SUMMIT of **Nodice** (❸; **1h**). There is another shelter here and, from the

Pregasina and the Dos de Cala from Nodice (Picnic 21)

little balcony, a bird's-eye view of Pregasina in its cliff-girt position, high above Lake Garda. The commanding bulk of Monte Baldo forms the backdrop to this scene. (If you want an unobstructed view to the north over Riva del Garda, you must scramble up to the right of the shelter. *Take care,* as the whole of this summit area is riddled with trenches, holes, and natural rock fissures.)

The descent from here may be a little vertiginous for some; it is secured and not difficult, but you must be surefooted.* From the balcony carry straight on, ignoring steps up to the left, and walk down a rocky shelf, before turning sharp right on a rough path (more RED DOTS WAYMARKS). This leads to the top of the **Scala Santa**, steps hewn from the rock face across the cliff, with a protective cable to aid your descent. The steps end under a huge overhanging cliff beside more wartime shelters. Go through a large cleft in the rock and then follow the path away from the rock face, to reach the MAIN WAYMARKED PATH (4; **1h07min**).

Turn left here on ROUTE 422, descending a sometimes skiddy path to a fine VIEWPOINT AND PICNIC SPOT (5). Just below, you drop through a shallow gully and continue down to a junction, where you turn left. The path gradually widens to a track, later concreted on a very steep section. At the bottom of this, at another junction, turn left along a minor road to pass by the CHURCH of **Pregasina** (6; **1h35min**), with views over this attractive village to Monte Brione and Monte Stivo.

*To avoid this descent, retrace your steps to the WAYMARKED BOULDERS on **Bócca da Lé**. Turn left downhill to rejoin ROUTE 429 by the 'Scala Santa' junction (4).

Carry on by the old WASHING AREA and take the first fork to the right, downhill into the centre of the village. At a large water trough in a small square, turn left (notice, to the left, the window display of war material) and then bear right to meet the top of a cobbled path. Walk down this to the asphalt road and turn left. At the first bend, turn left along a narrow road which drops quite steeply alongside houses and gardens. The road deteriorates into a track and then joins the main road again, just opposite a large STATUE OF THE MADONNA (7). From here there are superb views over Riva del Garda and Torbole and down to the next section of the walk — the old road to Pregasina.

Continue down the road to the entrance to the new TUNNEL (**1h52min**).

Here turn sharp right, through a gate, to walk on the old road. This is a superb piece of engineering, but we suspect that the residents of Pregasina rate the tunnel more highly! The road twists down the rock face, with sharp hairpin bends, but at no point is it steep and there are wonderful views all the way. The old route from Riva del Garda to Lake Ledro can be seen on the opposite cliffs.

After about 20 minutes, look for a path that intersects the road. Here, turn left to take the upper path, which has a wooden handrail. You rise up on an old cobbled mule track and pass a SHRINE. The path levels out and follows an electricity line. Note the old wayside stone erected in 'Anno Domino 1746'. Pass an information board about the local environs (in English) and then keep left on the upper track. You go under an archway and reach the new road again at the other end of the tunnel. Turn right here to meet the JUNCTION east of **Biacesa** (1; **2h35min**).

Index

Geographical names comprise the only entries in this Index; for other entries, see Contents, page 3. **Bold-face type** indicates a photograph; *italic type* indicates a map. Both may be in addition to a text reference on the same page.